CU00706385

WIMBLEDON
CONFIDENTIAL

Patricia Edwards

Pen Press Publishers Ltd

© Patricia Edwards 2007

All rights reserved. No part of this publication
may be reproduced, stored in a retrieval system,
or transmitted in any form or by any means, without
the prior permission in writing of the publisher,
nor be otherwise circulated in any form of binding or cover
other than that in which it is published and without a similar
condition including this condition being imposed on
the subsequent purchaser.

First published in Great Britain by
Pen Press Publishers Ltd
25 Eastern Place
Brighton
BN2 1GJ

ISBN 978-1-906206-11-6

Printed and bound in the UK

A catalogue record of this book is available
from the British Library

Cover design by Jacqueline Abromeit

To Jon

with a mother's love

Acknowledgements

Writing this book has not been easy. I have however had 'a little help from my friends'. I would like to take this opportunity to say thank you to some of them.

My thanks to my husband Ian who has given me much encouragement and has helped me to keep my sentences short. To Charlie Sale of the Daily Mail for his enthusiasm and support throughout. To many of my assistants over 32 years of hard toil, especially the wonderful Annie Dickins, Ros Graham, Alison Gardener, Liza Williams*, Diana Burston, Peni Webber and Pat Quayle who converted all my staff to vegetarianism. Thanks too to my controllers, especially the 'fab four', Shelagh, Jenny, Morag and Fanny who manned (or hand-bagged) the Royal Steps courageously. To Brendan O'Brien* who used to calm me down when things were tough and Walter Brunn, the smoothest of them all. My thanks also to the drivers who worked so hard, it is hard to pick out particular ones over such a long period but there was always the 'A' team to hand when needed. In addition there was Mark Byron the actor who springs to mind, the little and big Alli's, Stanley N'Waka the British Olympic rower, also the cousin of Prince William who had the press fooled for a while which was fun. The famous ones, Marti Webb, Stephanie Laurence*, Martin Bashir, and the quiet ones who kept their heads down and got on with the job. Of course, the directors of my company for their good guidance and advice also deserve much praise, Kit Molloy*, Robin Webb, and my amazing son Jon. Thank you too to my other two children who worked for me at Wimbledon and suffered with me, Catrin and Steffan. I must not forget my accountants, who worked with me when I was a marketing psychologist all those years ago, Malcolm Sugar and Ron Elliot for their work and patience with me - a paid up dyslectic - while running my company. I would also like to pay my respects to George Holmes* for getting me into all this and to Tony Cooper* for setting me off on the right foot. My thanks also to Charles Shafer of Hertz for guiding me through a difficult period and to Janet Dicks for making me laugh. I must not forget to thank Chris Gorringe especially for the early days and the hospital visits, and Richard Grier for his guiding hand.

So many people have played such a large part in the transport service over such a long time and I apologise to anyone I have missed out. I would like to thank the All England Lawn Tennis Club for opening up many opportunities for me, and of course 'Hughie Green'* who has a lot to answer for...

* deceased.

About the author

Patricia Edwards was born and reared in Liverpool to a Yorkshire father and an American mother. Although an only child she had a foster sister, Davina, with whom she is very close. Thrice married Pat has been with her present husband, journalist and broadcaster Ian Edwards, for the last 21 years. They have three children and four grandchildren.

Pat's varied career started at the age of 3, when she appeared as a fairy in the pantomime Snow White and the Seven Dwarfs at the Blackpool Tower Theatre. She later attended drama school where she gained the LAMDA gold medal for acting and appeared on stage and in many television programmes and films in the 1960s. When her son Jon was born she retrained as a marketing psychologist. She then began a hugely successful business career where she became involved with the creating of the All England Lawn Tennis Club's transport department whilst working also on many other transport projects for different clients around the world. In addition Pat has continued to model and to appear on stage but more in the capacity of Fashion Show compere. She closed her transport company and retired in 2004 though she still retains her connections in the world of fashion. She gives her reasons for retiring as boredom at hearing such remarks as "What's a nice girl like you doing in a job like this!"

Foreword

Pat Edwards has played a central role during the Wimbledon Fortnight for more than thirty years. From 1972 (the year Stan Smith defeated Ilie Nastase in one of the most thrilling finals ever) to 2004, when Roger Federer got the better of Andy Roddick, Pat was in charge of the courtesy transport service that Wimbledon provides for the players, VIPs, Press, junior players and even the public.

To say that she knows Wimbledon, the All England Lawn Tennis Club and the players like the back of her hand would be an understatement. No-one else has been involved with the club as long as she has, and understands as well as she does how the tournament, the All England Club and the players all get along – or not – over that well-publicised Fortnight. No one else knows what really happens behind the scenes, on those mysterious committees where seedings are decided, matches are scheduled (do they, or do they not favour Tim Henman?) and invitations to the Royal Box are decided.

Having relinquished her role in 2004, Pat can now divulge the best stories that she was privy to, and reveal what she really thinks about some of the characters she knew. All the great and the good of tennis feature and some will wish they hadn't crossed her path quite so often!

Wimbledon Confidential is an extremely rare behind-the-scenes look at the most famous tennis tournament in the world, the most exclusive tennis club in the world and the most successful tennis players in the world. Pat Edwards spares no one's blushes as she serves up stories and opinions that have never been revealed before – the perfect recipe for all who follow the Wimbledon Fortnight.

The Silver Plate presented to the Duke of Kent to celebrate his
25 years as President of the England Lawn Tennis Club.

Chapter 1

HOW IT ALL BEGAN

It was all Hughie Green's fault.

I gave notice to the firm of psychologists for whom I was working and decided to go on a two-month break to Greece. It had been a good job but I was young and looking for a change. When I returned to London a friend asked me if I would give a temporary helping hand to his girlfriend in her office until I found a job in my chosen career. She ran an employment agency, but suddenly every member of her staff just walked out *en masse*.

Strange as this sounded, I was happy to be earning while I took my time to find something more appropriate. Her agency had just been bought out by Manpower whose Managing Director, Lance Secretan, went on to become one of the world's foremost thinkers and teachers of effective leadership. The contact I had with him through Manpower impressed me greatly, and he went on to become an ambassador to the United Nations Environment Programme and one of America's most sought-after keynote speakers, frequently addressing business audiences around the world.

I began to work for Girlpower, the Manpower subsidiary, and found the work quite trivial after my previous high-powered employment. I found I was merely placing people in temporary jobs. Many of these jobs were for people euphemistically called "personality girls" on short-term contract work.

My new boss discovered that fifty girls were being sought

by British Leyland Cars to work for them as drivers. She asked me to travel to Birmingham with her to try to win the contract. In 1972 an order for as many as 50 staff for two weeks was a contract worth pitching for. On arrival at British Leyland's premises at Longbridge, George Holmes, a senior manager, met us. We discovered he was no pushover when we began to promote our expertise and credentials for the job, because he made it plain that he would rather use male apprentices from inside the Longbridge factory to do the work instead. The project was for 50 people to drive at what was probably the first ever sponsored courtesy car service in the sports field. This job was to be at the All England Lawn Tennis and Croquet Club, Wimbledon, for the annual tennis Championships. However, after I hastily showed him the difference in costs between full-time apprentices and girl drivers (including loss of apprentice time), Mr Holmes was convinced and he allowed the contract to come our way. So far so good.

Having received confirmation that we had been awarded the contract, my boss lost interest in the project. "You manage it," she said.

In my previous marketing career I had been vaguely involved in scheduling on the London Underground – this was to stand me in good stead for the task ahead.

The next thing I had to do was meet the people who ran Wimbledon. It was an interesting prospect but not at all what I had envisaged. Tony Cooper, the Club Secretary, was absolutely charming and I liked him immediately. He took me into the Clubhouse for a drink. At that time, Club members could use the bar to pour themselves a drink. Tony made me the most enormous gin and tonic I had ever seen, the first sip of which made my eyes cross. He then showed me around the grounds, shook hands and I tottered back to my car. I was none the wiser as to what Wimbledon expected of me, but a genuine, long-standing friendship had begun.

As Wimbledon Fortnight drew nearer, (incidentally it is always held in the last week of June and the first week of July) we began to recruit staff. I decided that each candidate that was put forward should be given a short driving test by the British School of Motoring, because the passengers to be carried were important people. Three quarters of the personality girls recruited failed the test, though the BSM instructors hung around offering free driving lessons to the good-looking ones. We started recruiting again. Eventually we had a team of 50 girls who could actually drive.

As the tournament drew near the excitement in the agency was intense. Uniforms had to be made and drivers briefed. Mr Holmes asked for the whole team to collect their cars from Selfridges Garage, off Oxford Street, where they were being stored and to drive them to Longbridge, Birmingham for a press call to announce the British Leyland sponsorship.

We all duly arrived at Selfridges Garage and collected our vehicles. I had arranged that I should be the last to leave, to make sure they all got away safely. I had Veronica Smith as a driver who was later to marry the boxer John Conteh. All the drivers set off equipped with maps and wearing their uniforms for the photo shoot in Birmingham. Veronica and I followed in the last car as arranged. I relaxed as we drove along the M1, and we didn't see a single one of our cars along the way. Things were obviously going well. We found the factory at Longbridge quite easily and drove in, expecting to see all the cars there before us. However, there were no cars, only members of the Press and Mr Holmes. Consternation. The cars couldn't have broken down or we would have seen them on the way. Mr Holmes was apoplectic with rage and I had a sinking feeling in my stomach. We ended up with Press pictures of myself and the lovely Veronica posing by our car.

An hour later a couple of the other cars showed up and were also photographed. It appeared that they had all stopped off a couple of times for coffee, hair arranging and the renewing of make-up. This was my first taste of running a driving team and I learned very quickly that you were only as good as the people working for you, so you had to learn to choose them carefully, and just as important, how to control them.

Finally Wimbledon 1972 started. In those days it was a fairly low-key event, organised by gentlemen who had a talent for pouring large drinks. The American players nicknamed them "the guys with the ties". In the office allocated to me, next to the main Club entrance, known as The Royal Steps, was what was known as the booze cabinet. I was later to learn that every office at the Club was supplied with one. It was stocked as handsomely as the American Bar in the Savoy. There was, however, very little stationery, no proper telephone and an acute shortage of chairs. A field telephone was provided so that I could call for cars. I discovered, after some confusing answers, that the other end of the field telephone was draped over a tree in a field where the cars were parked. When all the cars were out, it appeared that some local ladies passing by, walking their dogs, often answered this phone.

There was, surprisingly, an incumbent Transport Manager, Ted Sherwood and his wife Ivy. For years their job had been to telephone the local limousine company whenever a top player needed transport to leave the grounds. Ted and Ivy were rather defeated by the prospect of 50 Morris Marinas with girl drivers.

For a while, black limousines continued to appear at the Royal Steps. George Holmes took a dim view of this. "Do something," he yelled at me. This was a difficult order for me, because the lady who had employed me would not let me out of our Bond Street office to sort things out in Wimbledon. The reason she gave was that she needed to keep appointments with her hairdresser and beauty salons during the day. I felt I was being torn in two. Every day after work I drove down to Wimbledon to try to sort things out. I realised that the cars were not being used properly and on some days not at all. Clearly, some kind of system was needed which would benefit both the Club and British Leyland. I burned the midnight oil trying to create a system that would keep both sides happy. I also felt that I should have been on duty at Wimbledon all day, or at least I should have appointed a deputy to follow my orders.

I devised a system using flight boards (similar to those used by the Royal Air Force) and tickets for bookings. I worked out likely schedules for the vehicles, and here my previous London Underground scheduling experience helped me. This was all done during the evenings and early morning before reporting to the Bond Street office. However, during The Championships everything was up and running and it was difficult to implement these changes. I kept my ideas for future reference. I was also cooking food for the drivers at home and taking it to Wimbledon in the evenings. It was exhausting and I couldn't wait for it to be over.

The final bombshell landed in the form of the Champions' Ball. In those days it was held on the middle Saturday of The Championships in Central London, and did not end until 2.30 a.m. What is more, I was expected to attend the event as a guest and this left no one to run to run the service. My boss, who had not put in an appearance, was not invited. The 50 drivers were very tired and I had no substitutes, nor was I allowed to look for any. Somehow, we muddled through. Many drivers fell by the wayside because the job was too demanding. They were being paid £8 a day with no overtime. I didn't blame them. I did realise that we needed to contract them should we do the job again, and try for a little more money or at least some overtime payments.

It had been a difficult two weeks, but I was about to return to my normal career as a marketing psychologist and had managed to line up two job interviews for the end of July. Wimbledon would become just a memory, or so I thought.

In August 1972 George Holmes telephoned me at Manpower. "We have decided to sponsor Wimbledon again next year, how do you think we should run it?" he asked.

"Well I can give you a few pointers," I replied, "but I won't be working on the account again as I am leaving Manpower to pursue my chosen career."

George was not a quiet man and he was horrified about my intentions. "But you were the only one who did any work!" he shouted. "Who would run it for us if you were not there?"

I was determined to stand my ground and not to work at Wimbledon again, but George continued to argue the point with me. "Alright," he said after several minutes' argument. "How would you feel about British Leyland setting you up in your own business by giving you the Wimbledon account and I'll throw in the Motor Show as well?" he added. I began to waver. The Motor Show was a big account, much bigger than Wimbledon in those days, and to start my own company with two guaranteed accounts, and one as big as the Motor Show, was extremely tempting. I thought I could probably get some research work at the same time, as I found putting girls in temporary jobs extremely boring. In the end I gave in. I often wonder if I did the right thing.

As soon as everything was settled with British Leyland I realised that I did not have much time before the Motor Show in September to get everything set up. It promised to be a fairly hectic two months.

During the month I received another phone call, this time from Hughie Green, an old friend from my theatre days. "Would you do me a favour?" he asked. "I have a hairdresser in Jermyn Street who wants to do an act on *Opportunity Knocks* to prove he is the fastest hair cutter in the country." I groaned. "That sounds awful," I said. "Well," said Hughie, "I don't want to offend him and I need someone to announce him and his act. Someone who is used to working on television." (In my youth I had done a lot of television, some of it with Hughie.) It suddenly occurred to me that this might be a way to announce my company on the programme, as I didn't have much time to get brochures printed, let alone send them out announcing our opening. Why not announce it on television? There was a snag, however. Hughie at that time was working for the BBC, which meant he was dead against my idea because no mention of a commercial company could be made on air. After much argument, I agreed to appear on *Opportunity Knocks*, and Hughie agreed that we should ad-lib the announcement of my new company on air, although during rehearsals we would follow the script. *Opportunity Knocks* went out live in those days.

This sounded good to me, and it worked out well. The final outcome was that the hairdresser did not win *Opportunity Knocks*, but I made my announcement, and it brought me extra accounts. At the same time Hughie had fulfilled any obligation he had to his hairdresser.

So Promcat, as the company was then called, was born. Incidentally, that name changed to Gemini Two International Ltd in the late '80s, when the whole company changed its structure too.

In 1973 I was back at Wimbledon, working for myself, and the first thing I did was set up a proper transport system using my plans and observations from the previous year. The system I set up was used successfully, but with modifications I made over the years, until I left in 2004.

I copyrighted the system that had been planned and executed in my own time. I had not received any payments for the time spent creating it, either from my then employers Manpower, nor from the All England Club, so it belonged to me. An outsider employed directly by the Club later computerised my system, with my help. I understand that he later copyrighted the computerised version.

Chapter 2

PLAYERS AND THEIR GAMES

The year I started working at Wimbledon with my own company
was not the easiest year to choose. It was the year commonly
known as the year of the boycott by more than 70 men players.
They did this on the instructions of the Association of Tennis
Professionals (ATP) following the suspension by The
International Federation (ILTF) of the Yugoslav player Nikki
Pilic. This did not, however, appear to reflect on Wimbledon as
the crowds still came to see matches and it opened up the game
for less well-known players.

The final Saturday of the year before, when I was still gain-
fully employed by Manpower, had been rainy, which had washed
the games out. This meant that the finals were held on the Sunday for the first time, which caused mayhem for my driving
team and a lot of other people as well. My assistant, Annie
Dickins, and I took full advantage of this occurrence and viewed
a number of the finals matches from the Royal Box, as this was
not being used on the Sunday. Although I was invited officially
to the Royal Box in 2005, I was unable to take advantage of the
invitation. My would-be hosts would have been surprised to
know that I had actually sat in it already, in my jeans with a
large gin and tonic to watch the Ladies' finals.

Not only was all that happening but what a Men's final it
was in the year of 1972. It turned out to be one of the classic
matches on the Wimbledon calendar and was between Stan

Boris Becker in disguise with Pat and Ian Edwards (also in disguise) in Qatar.

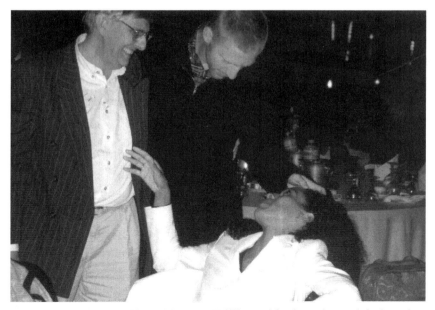

Boris and Barbara (wife) with Jerry Williams (sky broadcaster) in happier days.

Pat Edwards having dinner with Thomas Muster and friend in Qatar.

Pat Edwards in Qatar with the players - Arab style.

Steffi Graf poses with the Ladies' Plate.

Pat and Monica Seles (feeling the cold) at Hampton Court.

The Williams sisters with their courtesy car driver.

Boris Becker, John McEnroe, Bjorn Borg and Stan Smith leave the stadium after Millennium Parade

Andre wins the Men's Singles, Wimbledon.

Pat with Andre and Phil Agassi after Andre's win.

Pete and Lindsay at the Champions' Dinner.

Fred Perry with 80th birthday baloons.

Pat Edwards applauds Pete Sampras with Frew McMillan and Ricky Morea.

Pat demonstrates her system at Wimbledon to would-be new drivers, 1998.

With Ted Tinling and Richard Berens in Philladelphia.

Nadeem kidnaps Michael (Stich).

Smith, a lanky American, quiet and an honest craftsman, and the unruly, quirky newcomer a brilliant artist, Ilie Nastase from Romania. George Holmes of British Leyland had only let us use eight of the fifty cars on that unplanned finals day, as the other 42 cars were booked to be loaded on car transporters and sent back to Birmingham on the Sunday morning. Factory drivers were arranged from Longbridge to collect and return the remaining 8 cars when the games finished. This would be an expensive operation that did not please George. Eight cars should have been enough as British Leyland had agreed with the All England Club that a competitor would be allowed a single seat in a courtesy car to take him/her to their scheduled match and home again. Tennis players were to share cars. In those days, drivers went off duty at 1 p.m. and came back on shift again at 5 p.m., finishing at 9.30 p.m. working a single broken shift. This was to change radically as time went on but at that time the players had been told this was what was on offer. As this was the first time they had had the luxury of a courtesy car at Wimbledon it did not seem so bad. But to use an expression of my mother's, "much wants more" and in this case my mother was right.

Nastase lost the final, after playing a terrific game of tennis that had been a joy to watch. It had been arranged when players wanted their car home after their match that they waited at the Royal Steps. These Steps lead up to the entry to the Clubhouse which is the ivy-clad building we are all used to seeing on television. It is the entry also for Royals and dignitaries who can access the Royal Box that is positioned directly behind the building. The players' dressing rooms were also in the building so it was a convenient place to congregate and get into the cars. Our transport office was situated to the right-hand side of the Steps and Chris Gorringe's office was next to it. Later these two offices were destined to be knocked into one to make an office for the Club Secretary.

After winning the final match Stan Smith quietly got into the first available car seat to his hotel before Ilie arrived. When Nastase did arrive he had 'half of Romania' with him. He was told the last car (which had waited for him) had one seat left. This was for his use only. His luggage was by now being stowed into the car boot. He then started what was to be one of many of his performances at Wimbledon. He ranted and raved, played to the admiring crowd who had gathered to see the players leaving, and he refused to get in the car unless the other three player occupants got out and his friends got in.

Annie Dickins and I looked at each other in dismay. This was our first year at Wimbledon and we certainly did not know how to handle the situation. The committee members on duty had vanished, presumably to the bar upstairs, or were at least nowhere to be seen and dear Chris Gorringe hadn't even started working at Wimbledon in those days. The other players in the car were not about to give up their seats for Ilie's entourage to use and were all watching with interest. So with a heavy heart I did the only thing possible, and something I did not wish to do to someone who had played such a magnificent match and lost.

I told Nastase it was, as we say in transport parlance, "either rubber wheels or rubber heels". So Ilie, the loser of the match, unpacked his luggage dramatically from the car boot and he and his friends trudged dejectedly towards the main gate and a trip on the Underground (Tube) back to their hotel, while I was left with a crowd of people booing me and looking very threatening. Great, I thought. I do not remember feeling so bad before that incident and my heart went out to that receding figure with his slightly bowed legs and shock of dark unruly hair, carrying his tennis bag over his shoulder as he headed for the gate. I was not to know on that day that I would face an almost identical situation involving Cliff Richard many years later. However, I had become stronger by that time and was able to deal with things in a less emotional way.

In the following years, as Nastase worked his way through The Championships we got to know his moods well. Stanley Hawkins, who was then on the committee told me that he had once caught Ilie dancing naked round two of his rackets in the men's dressing room. "He's not all there," Stanley said but I had to disagree. He was 'all there' and his playing over the years was second to none. I can never understand why he was not made a member at Wimbledon. He gave so much pleasure to the audiences over the years and was one of the first personalities to bring in the big crowds to tennis.

Another player, Jimmy Connors, who in those days travelled with his mother Gloria, also caused ructions at the Club. Gloria thought she could take the courtesy cars anywhere, so long as Jimmy was in them. She always wanted to go to the launderette, the bank, the supermarket for Jimbo, as she called him. Later she got really ambitious and requested trips to Harrods or the hairdresser. She was very put out when I had to tell her the cars were for the players' use not hers – unless she was accompanying Jimmy to Wimbledon.

By this time I had managed to persuade George Holmes to change the rules to one seat for the player and one travelling companion, which made more sense. George agreed to this but would not supply any more cars, although there were potentially twice as many people now travelling.

I had to change the scheduling and although it was very tight to operate we managed for several years on 50 cars. Gloria used to scream "Jimbo" every time Jimmy played a point and the match officials asked her to keep quiet. I think it caused some embarrassment to Jimmy, although many would say he is not easy to embarrass. I think he blotted his copy book with the Club because he did not behave as they felt sporting gentlemen should. I am told that on one occasion after winning the Championships he attended the Champions' Dinner and was placed, as is the custom, on the top table, reserved for the two singles winners and all the Wimbledon dignitaries. Quite a few winners who have been given their place at the top table do not enjoy the meal without their friends around them. A lot of the players are young and not from privileged backgrounds so do not know how to handle this social occasion. On this particular evening Lady Burnett, wife of Sir Brian Burnett, the Chairman of the Club, saw Jimmy turn his fork to pick up his peas and gave him a withering look. Whereupon Jimmy used his knife to flick peas at her.

I remember years later when he had finished playing at Wimbledon he came to see me and brought his little son to meet me. "I was a bad boy in those days wasn't I?" he asked. I laughed and said, "Yes you were, but you did have a lot of charm and fun in you, although the Club did not see it that way. I am not as fond of the young players of today as I was of you lot then." The players towards the end of my career at Wimbledon appeared to me remote, perhaps because I had so much to manage I did not see them as much.

Another player to make problems, unintentionally, was Bjorn Borg. His appearance at Wimbledon started the saga of the teenyboppers who caused near riots on the grounds of the Club. Bjorn was quiet and unassuming at first and I can remember when he first made an entrance at the Royal Steps after his win in the finals. The place erupted with schoolgirls, screaming as hard as Beatles' fans, and surging forward to try and touch him. Bjorn backed off and disappeared into the Clubhouse looking white and shaken. I realised it was my job to get him out of the Club safely and back to his hotel so I asked the policeman on duty to try to hold back the crowds while we did something quickly. I decided on a decoy car that Annie Dickins organised which drove up to the Royal Steps and waited. The crowd thought this was Bjorn's car and they waited, the tension growing.

Meanwhile I took Bjorn via the ladies' loo at the side of the building where there was another car waiting to take him home. At the Royal Steps meanwhile the crowd had become impatient and started attacking the driver, who in hot weather had the car windows open. The poor girl was pretty with long hair that the schoolgirls kept pulling. They also pinched her in fits, I suppose, of jealousy. She was in tears and the policeman had to get in the car with her, close the windows and get her off the premises. The following year the Club erected barriers in front of the Royal Steps, which helped enormously, although I have witnessed the early barriers being knocked over, and the crowd surge forward after poor Bjorn and others.

Until Chris Evert came on the scene, Billie Jean King had been the Queen Bee of the tennis courts. Chrissie was around at the same time as Evonne Goolagong and they often came into my office for a chat. Chris would look out of my office window to see if Jimmy Connors was around and subsequently they became engaged. She was very smitten with Jimmy at the time and I remember the year they both became Champions at Wimbledon. They were newly engaged and in love, and at the Ball that year they opened the dancing (as it was usual for the male and female Champions to do). It was very romantic, they looked wonderful and there wasn't a dry eye in the house.

A strange incident happened with Evonne Goolagong, who was runner up to the Ladies' Champion in my first year at Wimbledon, when she met a young man named Roger Cawley. Evonne had been very much under the thumb of her trainer, who had virtually brought her up. When she met Roger they became serious about each other and her trainer was unhappy about this as he felt it would interfere with Evonne's career. When Roger and Evonne married against her coach's wishes she and Roger decided not to give Wimbledon their correct address in case he tried to contact them. All players are forced to give an address when they enter the Wimbledon Tournament. The only people who know the players' addresses are the transport service, for obvious reasons, and now the player liaison office. Neither I nor my staff have ever divulged this confidentiality to anyone else and I am pleased to say that we had the confidence of the players for all the years I was managing transport at Wimbledon.

On this occasion Evonne was due on court and had not ordered her car. I rang the number she had given to remind her but it was an unconnected number. If she didn't arrive for her match it would be cancelled and she would be out of the tournament, and none of us wanted that to happen as she was a great favourite at Wimbledon.

I had a brainwave. I thought I knew how to reach her and I told the referee's office not to worry – yet. My ex mother-in-law had been engaged to Roger Cawley's father in Hong Kong before the war. So I rang Malta where she lived and told her of the situation. "Oh he is still in Hong Kong I believe, how exciting, I'll try to reach him." She telephoned Roger's father, who rang Roger, who rang me, and the situation was saved. Evonne and I joked we were sort of related at a distance.

In 1985 a new face appeared on the scene. Boris Becker, freckled, with ginger hair and only 17 years old. He was a respectful young player, and he remained so during all his years at Wimbledon. On his first appearance at Wimbledon he came into the transport office and registered for a courtesy car, as all the players did. He was keen to do the right thing so he registered early. To put him at his ease I said, "You are the first player to register with us this year. Your ticket number is 1, I guess that means you are going to be Champion." He smiled at me, crinkling his piercing blue eyes. How prophetic my remark was! At the end of the Fortnight he was indeed the Champion, beating my friend Kevin Curren in the final. Poor Kevin had had to play Edberg, McEnroe and Connors to get to the final, only to be beaten by a 17-year-old. Life is sometimes very hard.

Boris married a beautiful black girl, Barbara Feltus, a model in her native Germany. Barbara was to become a real friend after we met at the newly formed Tennis Open in Qatar on which both my husband Ian and I were advisers in our own capacities. Boris was their star turn and the organiser of the event, Ali Alfardan, decided we should all be clothed in (expensive) Arab national dress. Not only that, we should all ride camels. The nearest Barbara and I ever got to that was to go to the camel racing, but we had a marvellous time each time we visited Doha (capital of Qatar) and we certainly became familiar figures in the gold souk. Doha gave me a wonderful chance to meet and mix with the players on a more sociable level than my job or the players' schedules allowed at Wimbledon. This led to a much better understanding of their needs and the limitations set by the Club on my job. I was sorry to see Boris and Barbara end their marriage, as they had been a remarkably close couple. Barbara and her mother, Ursula, were such fun people to be with that I am disappointed to have lost touch with them.

Another Wimbledon Champion visitor to Qatar was Stefan Edberg. Both Stefan and his wife were quiet people and I adored their tiny daughter who as a small baby did not have much hair. However she was a real tennis fan and, at about four months old, wore a pink sweat-band round her little bald head when she was taken by her mother to sit in the player's box and watch her father grace the tournament for so many years.

Stefan told me he intended to start a tennis school, coaching youngsters in Sweden when he retired from competitive tennis. I imagine we will be seeing a lot of gifted Swedish players descending on London and trying their hand at Wimbledon. Let's hope they are all as handsome and appealing as Stefan is.

While in Qatar I met Thomas Muster. Thomas had only played Wimbledon a couple of times and he did not wish to do so again. He was considered number 1 in the tennis world and was a very mature, strong character. While we were in Doha, when Thomas was playing, the Duchess of York was also a guest of the Qatar Tennis Federation. There was a rumour doing the rounds that they were having an affair and she was chasing him around the world. From my observations and from what Thomas told me, I think this rumour was untrue. I was there and so were the Press and it did make a rather good story.

Thomas impressed me greatly. He was in the top half of the top 5 in the world when at the Key Biscayne tournament, he was unloading his bags from the boot of a courtesy car when a drunk driver backed into him and trapped his legs into the back of the courtesy car. Doctors told him that he would be lucky to be able to walk again. Well he did walk again and he went on to regain the position in competitive tennis he had achieved before his accident. "Did you sue?" I asked him over dinner one evening. "You bet I did," he replied. I think overcoming such a serious accident, enduring the mental and physical pain and the long rehabilitation. and to play competitive tennis again takes real guts and I have a great admiration for him.

Another great household name and one who caused untold grief for the authorities at Wimbledon in the early 80's was Big Mac himself, John McEnroe. His was the confidence to be playing in a junior tournament at Wimbledon while trying to qualify for the main draw, and he did it.

From my point of view the junior players always travelled in a small bus as they were guests of the All England Club who paid for their trip. John had entered as a junior so he was put in the bus with the rest of them. Knowing that seniors were allowed a seat in a car, and he had just qualified (unbeknown to us) as a senior, he got out of the bus and took a seat in a car. My controllers, not knowing he had qualified, tried to move him out of the car, to no avail. I was called. I told him the junior rule and he said, "Yes, but I have just qualified."

Juniors had been known to do anything to travel in the cars with the 'big boys' so I was unsure that this was true and I said something along the lines of I would have to check and I would appreciate it if he would travel in the bus until I had been officially informed of his change of status. He was having none of this. An argument ensued during which I became fairly angry and banged my hand on the side of the car he was refusing to vacate. He put his hands around his head and said, "Don't give me a hard time, lady." I realised how very young he was. "Woe betide you if you are having me on," I said, allowing him to travel in the car. Of course, he was right and was in the main draw.

I came to realise John was only obstinate or rude when he was right. He caused so much trouble on the court through indignation that no one saw his point of view. I grew to like and respect him enormously and was very sorry for him during his marriage to Tatum O'Neal.

I was very touched when I heard he had said to Andre Agassi before his marriage to Brook Shields, "Think about it before you do it, there is only room for one star in a family." Sadly Andre's first marriage went the way of John's.

John is doing extremely well now as a television commentator and I wish him well, he is a most interesting character. I always felt sorry for his younger brother, Patrick, another excellent tennis player. Once when we were in Philadelphia for the US Open Indoor Tournament I stupidly said to Patrick how pleased I was that John was the Champion of Wimbledon. Patrick looked at me and said, "I was Champion at Wimbledon too this year. I won at doubles, aren't you pleased about me too?" Of course I was, but I think we all notice the singles champions more than the mixed or doubles champions, which seems a shame as to win Wimbledon in any of their competitions is the jewel in any tennis player's crown.

Pete Sampras, or 'Pistol Pete' as he was known, was a player who dominated Wimbledon for eight years. He was a fairly quiet boy when I first came across him in the Philadelphia

Open Tournament, which was the second largest US tournament in the country. He had been training at Nick Bolletieri's tennis camp with Andre Agassi when they were both very young.

Rumour has it they did not get on. As a very young player he was incredible to watch and of course he went on to do so well in this country. He was an approachable character and one day when he was driving into Wimbledon one of my drivers, Janet Fenton, had the sun roof open to keep the car cool in the heat of the day. As they were driving along a pigeon flew overhead and decided to make a comfort stop. It christened Pete, much to Janet's amusement. "It's supposed to be lucky," she said. Small comfort for Pete before a big match. It must have been lucky, however, as Pete won that day and Janet, the poet laureate among drivers, wrote a poem about it which she presented to Pete. Rumour has it that Pete had it framed.

Another thing I remember about Pete in his early days at Wimbledon was that I was asked to pick up formal evening clothes for the winning players who wanted to go to the Champions' Dinner. I was given sizes and the drivers went to collect the selections. The lady players chose their dresses and the men were issued with dinner jackets. I was the only one of my staff who attended the dinner and saw them all dressed up for the party. One year as the players appeared at the dinner Pete walked in wearing a pair of trousers which were too big for him. He is a very tall man so goodness knows what size the suppliers had sent. I spent the whole night worried that he might trip up in them. Fortunately for me and the Club he made it safely to the end.

My favourite of all the players was Andre Agassi. Andre was very flamboyant in his choice of tennis clothes, mainly because he told me Nike (his sponsors) chose the clothes for him to wear. The first time he played at Wimbledon he was not noticed much as he left quite early in the tournament. The time he came to my notice was the second time he played there, although I had watched him play in Vienna in the US Davis Cup team when he was wearing quite a get-up. When the speculation if he would conform to the all-white code of tennis dress demanded by Wimbledon was rife, we were all agog as to whether he would play at all or if the All England Club would ban him if he didn't. Either way he was certainly making a splash. I was not expecting the nice, polite person who entered Wimbledon that year. Another Bolletieri prodigy, he entered the arena in style with quite an army of supporters. In addition to Nick himself, Andre was travelling with his brother Phil, another good tennis player, Gil, his bodyguard, after whom Andre later named his son, an IMG official and a best friend from his school days. He also had a sweet girl Wendy in tow, who was his childhood sweetheart. They were a very friendly and endearing crowd of people.

The year Andre won Wimbledon was an incredible one for transport. Everyone in my department adored Andre, particularly one of the telephonists who was a very ardent fan. I told Andre this and he went over to her place of work and planted a big kiss. The girl went very pale and sat there with her mouth open. She was so overcome with emotion I had to send her out for some fresh air. I doubt she washed her face again for the rest of the tournament.

Andre gave us all tee shirts to wear on the day of the final, which was against Goran Ivanisovic, who everyone thought would win. Andre said he felt better knowing my transport staff were all behind him and told me not to worry about Goran's big serve. "I am the best returner in the business," he said. "I hope so," I replied, "I just want you to return with a big silver cup full of sparkling liquid." He laughed and promised to do just that. And he did.

When the match was over I had a phone call from Andre's brother Phil asking me to take Wendy, Andre's girlfriend, over to the Royal Steps. She had been watching the game from the television in my office and was in quite a state. As I feared a car would be mobbed, I decided to walk Wendy over as I was sure we would be quicker and reasonably unrecognized that way. When we arrived Wendy went straight into the waiting courtesy car by the Royal Steps. Andre asked me to wait with him and help him with his bags of gifts. "And the cup?" I asked. "You bet!" he replied. There are pictures of me standing on the Royal Steps with Andre's arm around me holding the cup. It was the most emotional Wimbledon I have ever experienced. When we joined Wendy in the car and attempted to leave, the crowd pushed around our vehicle and it was quite scary. "What do they want?" asked Andre. "Your body," I replied.

Fortunately we had one of our police drivers taking us back so I knew we would be safe enough. When we got to the transport office in Somerset Road the drivers were out on the pavement cheering our hero en masse. Andre, Phil, Nick Bolletieri (who was in tears of joy and kept saying "I have waited so long for this"), Wendy and the IMG people were all hugging and kissing and the drivers posed for pictures with them all, as did I. It was a really happy occasion and it made Wimbledon worthwhile for those drivers involved in it.

Andre went on to be a unique competitor although on one occasion when he had the first match on Centre Court his car was turned away by the security staff manning the gate and told to enter by another gate which made Centre Court inaccessible. The driver with Andre came back to transport headquarters. He was very upset and worried that we would not be allowed into the grounds that his concentration was going. I jumped into the car with him and went back to the main gate. "Open up this gate immediately!" I shouted, "this is Andre Agassi and he is first match on." The young security officer said, "It wasn't me who wouldn't let him in it was the Police." The policeman directing traffic opposite shouted over, "No it wasn't, it was security." "I don't care who it was, just open the gate!" I shouted, which they did. There always appeared to me to be friction between the security and the police and on this occasion it nearly stopped the first match on Centre Court.

Another occasion which causes me to smile was when Barbra Streisand came with fashion designer Donna Karan to visit Wimbledon to watch Andre play. Of course there was intense interest in an older woman and superstar coming to see a young champion and the Press were everywhere. Until the game Andre needed somewhere for Barbra and Donna to sit in peace away from the spotlight. He brought them to my office.

My office at Wimbledon was in those days a complete shambles. Transport is never considered by the people who run sports events until the last minute. We are usually stuffed into some cubby-hole that no one else wants. We were using the Link building which links all the covered courts and was not built as offices. Apart from a kitchen and four cooks, 300 staff were also in there, and my office and my assistant's office were just partitioned boxes. Not a place I would have chosen to entertain a superstar.

The ladies were with me for about half an hour and we chatted, drank coffee, and I showed them around. I was very struck by Barbra's hair. It was so beautiful, I had never noticed when watching her films, how really lovely it was.

When they decided to leave, Barbra asked me to check for fans outside. There were none as they didn't know where she was. She and Donna nevertheless crept out, with me following, also creeping, until we reached the car. Still no fans, and why was I creeping I wondered. They got in the back of the car and sat on the floor. This was presumably so the fans (who were nowhere to be seen) would not see them as they drove through the streets.

I was quite amused by it all and we must have looked ridiculous. However it was a great thrill to meet them both. I have always loved Donna Karan's clothes, I think she is one of the best designers there is. Of course Barbra makes just the best music, so it was a great treat for me.

Not all tennis stars are as kind as Andre, and many lose their way due to crowd adoration. When I met Tim Henman for the first time it was in Qatar, at their tournament the first ATP tournament of the year. Warren Jacques who had been coach of our Davis Cup team, had first tipped Tim as a player to watch when the LTA showed no interest in him. Warren took Tim to Australia to give him a chance when he was quite young and Warren told me to look out for him in Qatar.

As luck would have it one evening I found myself sitting at the same table as Tim for dinner. I introduced myself and we chatted. He appeared to me to be the epitome of an English gentleman. He was clean cut, well mannered and able to conduct himself socially, a skill which a lot of players don't have. It augured well, I thought, for England's chances of finding a Champion.

Of course we have had some other wonderful contenders for The Championships since Fred Perry won in 1936. Roger Taylor, John Lloyd, Buster Mottram and Jeremy Bates, to name but a few, all of whom raised our hopes of winning the Men's Singles, but were thwarted. Maybe Tim would be different, I thought, he was certainly an outstanding player and what an ambassador for Britain. Much later I was to become very disappointed in him. As Tim's fame rose, he became more aware of himself and his position in the world wide tennis arena.

One day during Wimbledon, I was approached by a television company who said the Wimbledon press office had given them permission to follow a driver for a day to see what the driving job was all about. Of course, as this had the Club's blessing I could only acquiesce. To choose the driver for what would be a very sought after job, my company Gemini Two decided the job should go as part of a prize for the driver who had won our 'driver of the week' competition.

The winner that week had been a young lady. In my system each time a player telephones in for a car, the next car available on our dispatch board was called to do the job. There was no favouritism for either driver or player.

The driver's name was called, the driver went to the desk, collected the car keys, a journey ticket and set out. As luck would have it when Tim rang for his car, the next one due out was that of the driver with the television crew following her. I had insisted that the crew travel in their own car and had no contact with any passengers. A general whoop from the other drivers and much clapping as the blushing driver rose from her seat when her car number was called and headed for the desk where a controller handed her the car keys. The television crew were thrilled too as this would make their film a lot more interesting. Off they all went in convoy and as the morning wore on we thought no more about it.

Later I received a personal phone call from a furious Tim complaining that I had sent a television crew to his home to interview him. I was shocked as this was certainly not the case. Tim was not at the centre of the film to be made and no one had approached him. He just assumed that he was the important one. I was quite angry too, although I apologised if it had upset him but explained it was the Club who had instigated it, and the centre of attention was focused on the girl driver not him, although I admitted that because his name had come out of the hat as it were, everyone had been pleased.

He calmed down and agreed to get into the car but would not let the television crew film it. Not long afterwards I received a call from Chris Gorringe telling me to apologise to Tim, who had telephoned Chris, and complained about it after he had spoken to me. "I already did," I said, "on behalf of the Club for any misunderstanding. "Oh," said Chris, "Well he has complained

31

to me and to his agent at IMG, perhaps you should apologise to her too." "No," I replied firmly. "I have already apologised to Tim so he would not be upset before his match only to discover he was coming in to practise. I am not prepared to apologise to anyone else for this. Perhaps the Club should apologise to my driver who was trying to do her job and was torn off a strip by Tim, which really upset her."

This was the last I heard of that little tantrum but it did not endear me to Tim and I was not best pleased with the Club's reaction, whose idea it had been in the first place. However I would be more than pleased to see Tim win that coveted cup and bring home the bacon for England. Transport do more than 2000 pickups daily over the Wimbledon period and if you get one wrong there is hell to pay. No one at the Club, however, thinks to say thank you for the 1999 successful pickups though.

Although Andy Murray was not around while I was at Wimbledon I have watched his progress with interest. He reminds me very much of Fred Perry and if he does half as well as Fred did then he will do alright. I think it is his lack of favour with the establishment which will stand him in good stead. He apparently does not take any nonsense from them, judging from the newspaper articles I have read about the criticisms he has made, which don't go down any better than Fred's did. He is outspoken and a very good player. I would very much like to see him holding the Men's Singles Trophy as well at Wimbledon and I am sorry I won't be around to see the reactions of the 'guys with the ties'.

There was another player who gave me a hard time early on in my time at the Club. He was very prominent at Wimbledon but shall remain nameless. I had been appointed as the AELTC'S transport manager in 1975 when Jack Sherwood retired. I was given a special badge which allowed me to go anywhere on the grounds, even the Royal Box, if the occasion demanded it. I was very proud of my tin badge with its crossed rackets. I was very proud of my new position although George Holmes hated the idea that I now worked for The All England Club (for a salary) as well as for him.

The nameless player in question bumped into me one day as I was doing my rounds of all the outposts of the transport office. He waved to me across the concourse and I waved back. I decided to visit the 'ladies' and cut off to the left before returning to my office on the Royal Steps. I entered the cloakroom and was making my way to one of the cubicles when I heard a noise behind me. I was shocked to see the player there, still smiling. "Get out of here," I said. "This is the ladies' room." "I just wanted to say hello," he said pushing me back, half into the cubicle. I tried to fight him off as he tried to kiss me and remove my clothes.

Luckily I was wearing a skin-tight leather trouser suit which was giving him a lot of trouble. I was very frightened and a terrific struggle ensued. As my suit was so tight and he was having zip trouble I was able to position myself and bring my knee into his groin so hard he bent double. I ran for the exit quickly and stumbled down the stairs, panting and dishevelled and made a dash for my office, where I slammed the door quickly. My assistant looked at me in amazement. "What on earth have you been doing, you look a real mess," she said. When I told her she roared with laughter. "You shouldn't wear tight leather with all this testosterone about," she said, unsympathetically I thought. Guess what she gave me to help me stop shaking? Oh yes, an eye-watering G & T. To this day the player, now a tennis coach, still waves to me cheerily whenever I see him. When he is around and I need to go to the Ladies I just cross my legs.

A more romantic liaison with a Wimbledon and US Tennis Champion followed a couple of years later in New York while I was still single. I was visiting the US Open and meeting my counterparts who ran the transport over there. They had liked the systems I had introduced to Wimbledon and I was helping them refine their own systems as they had been getting a lot of criticism at the time.

I was given a seat in the President's Box to watch the tennis each day which was very gracious of the USTA (United States Tennis Association) and which I really enjoyed and appreciated. Their president-elect was Randy Gregson. Randy and his beautiful wife Isobel, who had worked as a Christian Dior model before she married, took me under their wing and incidentally became lifelong friends.

They made sure I was invited to all the parties and functions that were being held at the Open that year and there were many exciting ones, such as dinner at 21 Club (fashionably known as 21) which I had only read about and was dying to see. The highlight of the fortnight, however, was the ball at a Park Avenue Hotel. I had a ball gown in my luggage (packed in hope) and I was very excited to be a Park Avenue princess for the evening. The only snag was I had to arrive alone as I didn't have a partner. "Oh don't worry," said Teddy Tinling (the fashion designer well known for the Gorgeous Gussie knickers he had designed for the tennis player Gussie Moran), who was dealing with the guests, "I'll put you on a nice table."

I hailed a taxi and arrived at the hotel which had steps leading up to the imposing entrance. As I ascended the flight of stairs, flashbulbs nearly blinded me and press photographers jumped in front of me anxious to get a photograph. I felt like a Park Avenue princess indeed.

As I entered the ballroom itself, across the gallery leading from the entrance which was over the dance floor, I was startled to see faces nearly at the same level that I was. I quickly realised that they were professional dancers on stilts on the dance floor. It was truly breathtaking.

The scene below was awesome. All the tables were awash with candles, flower arrangements and each had two large tennis rackets covered in sparkling stones crossed in the middle of each table catching the candlelight. The Americans certainly know how to put on a spectacular show. I found my table and was seated between two Champions both at the US Open and Wimbledon, one of whom introduced me to his wife, the other said he was alone. I was acquainted with both from their visits and fame at Wimbledon but did not know either of them well.

We all chatted as we enjoyed our superb dinner and the player who was single asked me to dance. He was as accomplished a dancer as he was a tennis player and we danced the night away. He told me that if I hadn't arrived he had been intending to leave after the Hall of Fame presentation. This is when all the American Champions go onto the stage to be applauded and the new Champions are welcomed into the Hall of Fame. After the ball we went on to a night-club and had a wonderful time. During my trip we became inseparable and had the most amazingly romantic time. Distance, however puts a damper on relationships and although we have kept in touch, that wonderful two weeks faded to a memory when we returned to our own homes and lives. We are still in touch to this day and my husband and I count him as one of our good American friends.

Although I had always known Ian Edwards (my present husband) we had merely passed the time of day at Wimbledon. In 1984 his wife died of cancer, just as I was going through a divorce. I will leave Ian to tell the story in his own words which were printed by the *Times* newspaper in a spoof copy produced in honour of John Parker's retirement, but first I think I should say that I had met John Parker at Wimbledon when he was reporting for ITN.

John Cotter of ITN, who had a disability and limped, had been working with Alan Zafer, George Holmes' replacement at

British Leyland (now called Austin Rover). John Parker arrived in my office for a car saying he was John Cotter. I looked at him, liked what I saw and as he was from ITN I thought I had better give him a ride home. I wrote a journey ticket with the name John Cotter then said, "Wait here while I get your car." I limped to the door. "Oh hell," he said, "You know John Cotter then." After that John Parker and I became good friends. Then he brought Ian Edwards into my office. I will let Ian tell the story as *the Times* spoof showed it.

"John (Parker) would be at the tournament until early evening, when he would return to edit and voice the item for *News at Ten*. It was my responsibility to edit and voice the item for the early evening news at 5.30 p.m. John realised how strong my enthusiasm for tennis was and asked me to visit Wimbledon, swapping roles for a day. He was about to leave for the office when he decided to introduce one more person, asking me to an office beside the Royal Steps, the Club's main entrance and saying, 'If you want a lift back to the office at the end of the day, here's the lady who'll organise it for you.' The Transport Lady, Patricia-Anne Banks.

Attractive, blonde, aged 37, Pat Banks took one look at me and wondered to herself, 'I've just got used to John Parker and I rather like him – but why does he have to bring this little squirt along with him?'

That was the first of 12 consecutive Wimbledons for The Little Squirt who in 1986 married the Transport Lady, and promptly resigned from ITN. The Little Squirt now works full-time at Wimbledon. Pat Banks is now Pat Edwards, attractive, blonde and still 37 and still The Transport Lady. Guess who came to the wedding? John Parker."

The following year I visited Flushing Meadow. Randy Gregson, as the president elect, was about to take office. When the last ball had been struck and the courts cleaned and emptied for the night, Randy, Isobel (his wife) and I entered the deserted arena and stood by the net of the American Centre Court and opened a cold bottle of French Champagne in the quiet moonlight. I was honoured to share that moment with them both. We toasted Randy, who went on to make a most marvellous president and of whom I was and remain very proud. I will never forget that magical moment when we toasted him in the moonlight.

Of course there are past Champions who visit Wimbledon, most of whom still have a fairly big ego of their own (deservedly) and who can be very entertaining and enormous fun to deal with. They have achieved a lot and feel confident about their personalities and they do not need to throw tantrums at the drop of a hat.

In the past, players were treated differently to today. They did not win as much prize money and there is still some resentment among them, today's players expect to have everything done for them and be paid a fortune if they reach the top. Of course, younger players are still struggling to survive on the international tennis circuit but not in the way that all players used to struggle in years gone by.

I have noticed that in the past, these older people have made friendships and even 'groupships'. For instance, the Australian players stick together and often in the evening they have what they call 'a sausage sizzle' in one of the houses where they stay for the duration of the tournament. This appears to be the older players – John Newcome, Fred Stolle, Ken Rosewall, Tony Roche, my friend Warren Jacques and others too numerous to mention.

This type of friendship does not seem to take place amongst the younger set anymore. The only time I can recall a more recent friendship of this kind was between Andre Agassi and John McEnroe. Maybe it wasn't that close but they did leave messages with me as to what time and where they were meeting in the evening. As I was the one who organised their comings and goings, it was a sensible place to leave a message in the hurly-burly of Wimbledon and I was happy to see it happening. The present players travel with their own entourage and tend to keep to themselves when the day's tennis is over.

Buzzer Hadingham fought long and hard when he was the AELTC Chairman to start up a social club where past players could meet. He called it The Last 8 Club. Players who had made it to the quarterfinals were able to go there and enjoy a drink and chat to people they knew from the circuit. At Wimbledon it is nice to know you have a place to do that, as even a place to sit can sometimes be a relief, and it is easier if it is private than having to meet in the public restaurants.

I once met Jeremy Bates in Qatar, an English player alone, competing in the first ATP tournament of the year. He did not appear to know any of the other players well enough to hit with them and he had no entourage with him, not even an LTA official. He needed someone to practise with and so I introduced him to an Australian player I knew which turned out well for both of them. I felt, though, that there should have been more support for Jeremy and that we were not doing enough for our British Squad, as the other countries appear to do.

One morning at Wimbledon, both Jeremy and Andrew Castle had said to me that it was impossible to find anyone at the AELTC to hit with, as in those days it was not encouraged for British players to practise there regularly, so it was impossible to find a partner on the off-chance unless you had scheduled someone to play with you.

Among the players, the Club had a reputation of not being particularly friendly, and they were very aware of the rarified atmosphere of privilege enjoyed by the members. By now, perhaps the Club has decided to make available a greater number of the many practice courts at Wimbledon, giving our current players first choice over the older and non-competitive Club members, although I doubt it. It should be friendly enough just to drop in and find people of your own ability to hit with.

Here are two encounters among many others that I and my staff have suffered from the attitude of Club members. Early one morning I drove into the Club grounds to the covered courts in Somerset Road to start work and I saw a man driving round the field in his car where we parked our courtesy cars. I thought this a little strange until I saw his little dog running after the car trying to keep up with it. I was horrified. Not only were the working cars all due to arrive any moment but the poor dog was obviously not enjoying his walkies.

I called over to the man and asked him who he was (this was before the days of tighter security) and did he realise that 50 cars were about to arrive to service The Championships and they were heading in his (and his dog's) way. I asked him very politely if he would mind leaving. He was at this moment right in the middle of the courtesy car park, blocking the way in. He looked at me in disdain and said, "I am a member." "I see," I said, not too happy with this information, adding: "I believe members use the car park next to this one, I wonder if you would mind taking your dog over there, and in the interests of safety putting it on a lead." He looked me up and down and said, "Go away, woman, I am a member and I can do anything I like."

Another bone of contention we had with Club members was that they insisted on driving into their parking spaces in the shortest way, even though this meant entering the area through the gate marked OUT. We warned them repeatedly about this and were told the members preferred to enter that way and that the Club did not wish to offend them. Of course the inevitable happened and one old boy was hit by one of the large Park and Ride buses as it exited at the same time that he entered through the wrong gate. He lost control of his car and hit two other parked cars as well as the bus. Luckily he was unhurt but he caused a lot of damage. Did the Club apologise and forbid the member to go against the Club's own traffic signs? Of course not.

Fred Perry, Britain's last Wimbledon singles champion, was quite a colourful character from the good old days, and we shared a lot of fun with him. His 80th birthday was a very special occasion. I celebrated it three times because in each country that Fred visited that year, he gave an 80th birthday party. When his party was celebrated at The Championships, unbeknown to the Club I arranged to have helium balloons with "HAPPY BIRTHDAY FRED" printed on them and we tied them to each of the 50 cars. Since our cars covered about 20,000 miles over the Fortnight, most of London must have known he was 80. Fred adored every minute of it.

Over the years I was fortunate enough to meet many famous people as well as tennis players. In 1977, the Queen's Jubilee year, there was a parade of past Champions to celebrate the Centenary of The Championships. The Queen came on Ladies' Finals day, which was quite something as I believe she does not like tennis. She is, however, the Patron of the Club and her father King George the Sixth was an extremely good player who competed in The Championships as a doubles player in 1926.

There was also a parade of Champions for the Millennium in 2000 and as always I had to arrange for all their travelling requests. To see them all again struck me how people change, grow older, become coaches, television commentators and personalities on the tennis circuit, write books, find civilian jobs or just stay at home. Though they come from many countries, I have found that if you belong to the tennis community there is always a friend or at least someone you know, wherever you travel in the world. Tennis is a very close family, once you have been part of it.

I have been lucky to meet such marvellous people, one of them being Kitty Godfree. Kitty was born in 1896 and continued to visit Wimbledon until her death in 1992. She had become the grand old dame of Wimbledon by the time I was lucky enough to meet her. She was a lovely person, very sweet and charming and grateful for anything you did for her.

One year she telephoned me to arrange a car for the LTA Ball on the middle Saturday. "And could you collect my gentleman friend first and then send the car on for me?" she requested. She then gave me the gentleman's name and address. "Will you be going to the Champions' Dinner also?" I asked. "Oh yes, dear," she replied, so I made a note of her friend's address for the following week.

During the following week she called and asked me not to forget her car. "Oh no, Mrs Godfree," I replied, "Of course I won't and I have your gentleman friend's address if you would like me to have him collected." "Oh no," she said, "I'm not taking him this time, I have a different gentleman friend I would like you to collect instead." Well, I thought, I hope at her age I would be able to pick and choose amongst my gentlemen friends to take me to the Ball! That is if I get invited to any parties at that age.

Another very old ex-player was Jean Borotra. He had been known in his playing days as 'the bounding Basque' and he had some very French habits. He spent quite a bit of time in my office, as he apparently was fond of the girls. He would kiss their hands and not know when to stop by going right up their arms and had to be pushed off when he got to the shoulder. If he hadn't been an old man, he would have had many a slap.

He was not popular at the Club because of suspicions of his association with the Vichy regime in France during the war, accusations that he strongly denied. But it was his Wimbledon activities that worried me most.

When he was alive we were employing an all-girl team of drivers and I had many complaints about him regarding sexual harassment. I was sceptical at first because of his age, although

I still had to take the problem seriously. One day however he went too far with me personally and I had be very firm with him. He quietened down after that, I suspect mainly because he married a rather austere French lady who fixed him with a beady eye when he went anywhere near another woman.

In addition to transporting these current players and the players of yesteryear we had other guests to look after. Wimbledon is regarded as the largest of the Grand Slams, although the others like to snap at its heels. It is accustomed to hosting the tournament for the largest number of guests as well.

Between players and guests (or VIPs as they were commonly known), the split was about 50/50 for the transport department. The Club encouraged people to come to Wimbledon from other tennis events to do their business dealings there. This was particularly the case concerning the directors of smaller tournaments.

As all the important players liked to attend Wimbledon, there were good pickings for the smaller tournaments to try to persuade the players to appear for them as well. In my early days at Wimbledon, Derek Hardwick, a respected committee member from a well known tennis family, used to warn us not to shorten any lists of visitors, however busy we were, because in his opinion this was one of the reasons that had made Wimbledon so popular. Anyone who was anyone in tennis wanted to be invited, and it was a marvellous meeting and dealing ground for everyone. Most of the visitors were really pleasant and appreciative of our efforts. Of course there were a few male VIPs that appreciated the fact that we employed girl drivers in the early days, and quite a few of the girls complained that the men came on to them in a manner that was more than just friendly.

There were others who felt the cars were there for their personal use and they would try to order transport to take them to meetings in central London. This could not be done because first and foremost we were offering a player service. At least in my book, the players were more important than anyone else at Wimbledon.

There was one rather large visitor from Nigeria who stayed way out of town and who ordered a car to his address each morning. While he was eligible to travel he was one of those visitors who took liberties with the girls. This was a nuisance and after many complaints I decided that we had better use male drivers only for him. This caused a bubble in the transport pipe, as we had to delay his car until there was a male driver available.

He complained on the telephone many times a day as he felt he was not being treated as he should be. One day he came in to see me to complain yet again. He was very large and overbearing and usually appeared in national dress. He fully expected to browbeat me into submission. "Don't you know I am very important?" he asked. I looked up at him wide-eyed. "Oh really, who told you that?" I asked innocently. He steered well clear of me after that, but continued to annoy all the rest of my staff.

There was a mature and very famous lady player who was taken ill during Wimbledon. She had a mother who was 80 who lived out of England in the player's home town. The player was taken into hospital and had a major operation during the tournament. She swore me to secrecy, as she did not wish the Press to get hold of the story and upset her mother should she read about her daughter's illness in the papers. The player had to appear on Centre Court with the rest of the Champions in 1977, as she had been a winner at Wimbledon. I did not know how she was going to manage to do it as she had been at death's door the day before the Parade.

Our courtesy car went and got her from her rented apartment which was miles away from SW19. Fortunately I had a doctor working for me as a driver at the time so I sent him to drive her to Wimbledon just in case she was ill on the way in. She made it, she did her walk with the others, her mother watched on the television, and no one knew she was ill at all. I had always admired her as a player, but my admiration for her courage knew no bounds. None of my staff breathed a word to anyone about it, which made me very proud of them. She became a great favourite with us all.

We often appear to have problems with fathers who travel with their young daughters and one who springs to mind is Jennifer Capriati's father. Poor Jennifer, he really kept her on a tight rein. Her mother was a very sweet and attractive person, and Jennifer was well liked by those on the circuit at that time. Mr Capriati, however, threw his weight around with the Wimbledon staff, and mine in particular.

The players at this time were still allowed a seat in a car and one guest travelling. However, if both parents wished to travel with their child, I stretched the rules and allowed the young player to have mum and dad with them. Mr C, however, had other ideas. He expected to use a seat in a car anytime, and go where he wanted.

One day he had been playing up about this in particular, and I was called in to talk to him. I stood at the door and tried to reason with him. In true Italian fashion he lost his temper. He picked up the large tennis bag he was carrying and threw it at me. Unbeknown to him, if anyone throws anything at me, I catch it. So I staggered a little but caught his bag in my arms. I threw it straight back at him and he staggered, as he was not expecting it. "Don't you ever treat me like that again," I said. He realised he had gone too far and apologised profusely. He did not bother us so much afterwards, and always made a point of speaking to me in a very polite way.

Not so Mr Dokic. He treated his daughter quite appallingly, and one day we really had a bad time with him. We had a phone call from Jelena asking where her car was, because it hadn't turned up. We had no record of her ordering one. Our records are quite precise and at this point we had a computerised booking system that showed no record of a call from her. Luckily we had a car in the vicinity that we diverted to collect her. It arrived, I believe, five minutes after the time she said that she had ordered it.

She, and her father, refused to get in it and instead hailed a taxi which they took to Wimbledon, with our car following. Mr Dokic stormed into my office and started screaming at me, poking me in the chest and calling me a 'bandit' and saying he had called the Press. There were several senior people present, including Committee Member Julian Tatum from Wimbledon, but the most effective was Georgina Clarke who looks after the lady players for the Women's Tennis Association and who was brilliant at handling the situation. However I noticed everyone was trying to soothe Mr D, and were allowing him to insult me without any protection at all. They were afraid Jelena would pull out of the tournament.

To add insult to injury Mr Dokic had, the previous night, dumped Jelena at Wimbledon after she had lost her match. Being very young, she had sat in our lounge crying nearly all evening. My controllers who were on duty were very sorry for her and even offered to give her a bed for the night. She couldn't get into the family's rented apartment as Mr Dokic had the key. We thought that the probability of Jelena forgetting to order the car, and her fear of her father's temper, had made her claim that she had, in fact, ordered the car. However, though we had no apology from anyone involved in the incident, Julian Tatum said it had been appalling, and that I should write a letter for him to give to the Chairman, to explain what had happened. He felt the Club owed me an apology. I did as he suggested, writing in my own words, which he then altered. But at least I was happy that the Club knew my staff had not made a mistake and that they had rectified the situation by diverting a car to cover the request, even though it had not been used. Another lovely day in paradise!

Not all the girls' fathers behaved so outrageously. One I was particularly fond of was Mr Seles, Monica's father. His English was poor, but he was one of the friendliest people I have met at Wimbledon, and I have no doubt as to why his daughter adored him so much. No wonder Monica is the lovely girl she is, because not only did she later lose her father, she was also stabbed on court as well. This was a terrible thing for a young girl to deal with, and yet she always had a ready smile and is a great fun person.

Another father, although a VIP one, was Graham Lovett. He worked so hard towards Sydney's Olympic Bid, and also for tennis in general, that he was a popular guest at Wimbledon. It was tragic that he died a year before the Olympics because he would have loved to see how successful it became. Graham had a daughter, Belinda, and he was very keen that she should be involved in some way at Wimbledon. He became a friend of my husband and I, and of course he asked me if Belinda could work for the transport operation. Belinda was just the sort of girl I liked to employ, but the only snag was that she did not know London's streets.

To work at Wimbledon, your knowledge of the city has to be almost as good as that of a black cab driver, if you are to make the grade. How could I employ her with no knowledge at all? She and Graham both assured me she was good at reading maps and that she would do her homework before she started. I never for one minute regretted taking her on. She did so well that she went on to drive for me at the London Economic Summit (G7) when it was held in 1991.

The Summit was without a doubt the most exciting job my company ever worked on. We were engaged by the Foreign Office to supply drivers for cars supplied by Rover and Jaguar, which was ideal for us as we worked continuously with these companies anyway. It was the first time the government had used cars on a promotional basis, rather than paying the hiring fee, so there were many teething problems. Having pioneered Wimbledon, I had learned to cope with this problem before.

As we were only contacted three weeks before the summit began, we very quickly had to put in systems for 12-hour shifts to enable us to transport the heads of seven states and their entourages. We also had to find drivers. We ended up using a lot of Wimbledon drivers and we had to interview extra numbers while we were running the tournament, so it was a very busy year for us.

To meet people like Mr Gorbachev and Helmut Kohl, to chat to Mr Mitterand and George Bush Snr. was an unexpected treat. It was also very exciting, if like me you are into politics. Once into the Summit we were asked to change from 12 to 24 hour shifts. This taxed us to the limit because we had to employ more drivers, put drivers onto night shifts (which they hated) and change already delegated team leaders (which they also hated).

We had just finished that year's Wimbledon, and went on to the Summit the week after. Starting it in a state of exhaustion, as is always the case after the tournament, over the course of the following week my assistant and I slept for only about 16 hours. We slept for a full week after it was all finished.

1995 saw another problem with a player, this time with the Jensens. Luke and Murphy Jensen were American doubles players. Rowdy and always a nuisance, they often called for cars and then did not get into them. Otherwise they wanted the car to take them somewhere else, and made a habit of being pests in general. They were, however, not unpopular and we sometimes had to smile at their antics.

Their mother was also a large statuesque woman who was not quiet, to say the least. In order to keep her happy we always let our smoothest operator in the departure marquee handle her. His name was Walter Brunn and he soon had her eating out of his hand. On this particular occasion, Murphy Jensen disappeared and did not turn up for his match. The Referee's office called us to see if we had seen him or transported him anywhere. The Jensens that year were staying in a house up the hill, within walking distance of the Club. As we hadn't seen him we assumed he had walked down the hill and must be on the grounds. Sometime later the Referee's office called for a car to take them up to his house to see what was going on.

The next thing I heard of this was from the media. They, for some reason of their own, said I had kidnapped him. Well, if I had been intending to kidnap a player, I can assure you it would not have been Murphy Jensen. The story then changed, that he had gone to sleep in the transport office. The media then began to hang around our offices and played with the idea for a while until someone told them he had gone fishing. I will never know where he went to, and we were never offered an explanation. It did, however, disrupt our day in transport but then we were used to that.

Chapter 3

THE COURTESY CAR DRIVERS

Over the years I have had the utmost admiration for the driving teams. Most of the applicants were unused to working shift hours or working with so many people at close range, which meant that our systems were very regimented. A lot of the later drivers had held very senior jobs before they either retired or were made redundant. I felt that it was difficult for some of them to adjust to this type of job but once they did, they were ours for life and at times it was like running St. Trinian's, as everyone fell into line.

The camaraderie between the drivers has always been a very large part of the job for them all and many friendships were forged. The older drivers also found themselves part of a team of people instead of living out their lonely retirement at home which seemed to give them a new lease of life. After the drivers had attended their training days, the penny mostly appeared to drop as the systems we had taught them turned from lessons into the real thing.

In Wimbledon you hit the ground running, and there is no time to make errors so everyone helped each other and just got on with it. Most of the drivers I have spoken to admitted they were terrified on their first night shift. This was when the cars lined up outside the players' exit, and the drivers waited for their cars to be loaded. There could be up to four different players put onboard and four different addresses to work out

The first Courtesy car team, 1972.

Drivers in Boaters with their Rover cars, 1977.

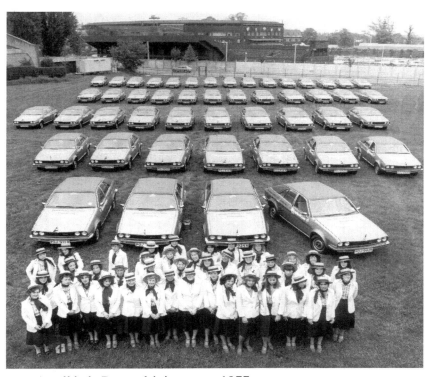

An all lady Rover driving team, 1977.

A colourful Wimbledon from Hertz - drivers in 1996.

"And for some it is all too much."

Another year, another set of drivers.

Pat Edwards with American USTA President Randy Gregson
at the LTA ball.

Controllers outside the transport office.

Pat Edwards is handed into her official car at Wimbledon by a
lady chauffeuse in 1980, the year of the Centenary celebrations.

The boy looks great but who are the hand maidens?

The new players building 2000.

before starting off, and this could be an ordeal in itself. There was an urgent need for this to be done quickly, because after their match players just wanted to go home and get away from the crowds. In addition to this urgency there were people milling about around the cars, disturbing drivers' concentration. Fans, officials, security personnel, stewards, staff, hangers-on and even Royal cars got in on the act as the poor drivers tried to plan their routes. It wasn't an easy job and on the first day of putting their training into practice I really felt for them.

Many drivers were also in awe of their passengers, who could range from famous tennis players, important officials, VIPs, film stars, and even on two occasions members of the Royal family. How impressive is that to a new driver? I was however amused to learn from one driver who told me that the passengers they were really terrified of driving were me and Robin Webb my co-director, who worked as vehicles manager during the tournament, and could be quite gruff at times. Still I suppose you have to be on your mettle when you drive the bosses.

The job the drivers did was quite demanding. There were periods of frantic activity with no respite, even for comfort calls, then periods of waiting until the next passenger requested a car, a wait that could be long and very boring. The job is well illustrated through one of driver Janet Fenton's poems – this one was entitled *The 1996 Effort*

Another year, another treat,
For a chance to sit in the driving seat.
Are we mad and a touch insane
To be back at this school again?

We can't do this, we can't do that
But we all try our best to please Robin and Pat,
We love it all – make no mistake
This team has spirit, hard not to fake.

Robin is here in his ten-gallon hat
He's quieter this year, well fancy that.
He's around to help when we get in a tiz
But can anyone tell me what Hugh's role is?

(Hugh was a manager working under Robin)

The uniform's not bad, but the skirt's a bit wide
Please can you tell me who else is inside?
Well, on to the car, the Galaxy's fun
But can anyone see where my wing mirror's gone?

The queue at the car wash at half past two
Gets us out of a run we may have to do.
The tricks are old – but we still do them now
Can anyone tell me who wants a trip to Slough?

We're at the marquee – we all sit and wait,
Which way shall I turn at the end of the gate?
Who will I get? What will they be like?
Will they be dressed in Reebok or Nike?

A trip to the Gloucester, Queens or St James,
A chance to drive some famous names.
That's why we do it year after year
And who can forget Lord Kindersley's cheer?

"Here we are again, happy as can be,
All good pals and jolly good company!"

Janet Fenton, June 1996

Janet was promoted to the job of Controller, so sadly we did not get any more of her brilliant poems, although her attractive presence on the transport players' desk made up for this.

As the poem illustrates, some drivers tried to work the system to their own advantage, but we had seen it all before and stamped down on these little tricks as best we could. The scam illustrated was for a driver to ask to fill the car up with petrol around 2 p.m. when the shift finished at 3 p.m. This way the driver hoped to avoid a long run which could spill over into overtime if they were in the Link building when a request came in.

Another was to lose their meal ticket and to beg a meal without it. About an hour later the same driver would suddenly find the ticket and hope to get a second helping. Often there were long visits to the loo or the driver would go to the smoking area outside and hope not to be called. However my Controllers were on the ball and most of the driving team were hard working, sometimes to the point where they wanted to be out all the time driving, leaving other drivers time to shirk. But unhappily for the shirkers, we were on to them too.

We had prizes which we awarded in front of the whole team to the 'driver of the week' and then to the 'driver of the year'. Usually they were token gifts, though in the latter years we had 'Best Driver of the Year' engraved goblets. These efforts went down well with the drivers who needed some recognition for the work they did. The Controllers who marked up drivers who had been willing and helpful during the working periods chose the winners. It was often very hard to pick which driver was the most deserving.

There was also a booby prize. One of our controllers had once done a sterling job at a previous event by washing up our coffee things in a makeshift kitchen. Despite the poor facilities he had insisted on wearing Marigold gloves to complete the job. We bought him a pair of rubber gloves with Marigolds and frills on the sleeves. Copies of these were available to give to any driver who merited a booby prize. The plan was for the booby driver to wear the gloves during a whole shift. We had to abandon this, however, as our Client was not keen as they were not exactly uniform!

The other perk of the job was a Gemini Two Certificate for 4 years trouble-free driving at Wimbledon. Our other jobs did not count on this, though some drivers who worked for us often thought that it should. The certificate guaranteed that the training days at Wimbledon would be shorter, and after four years these drivers only needed their knowledge brought up to date and a quick driving test to see if they had developed any bad habits over the previous twelve months.

All these team events helped to draw the drivers into one working team. Not easy on such a short job. Before the tournament began, the Controllers were given a special day for their efforts with a Champagne breakfast, a morning's run through what was required of them and a journey round all the different outposts. Each Controller explained the difficulties of their job from the previous year and how their colleagues could help overcome those difficulties, and then on to a good buffet lunch with wine and a gossip with old colleagues catching up on the year's news.

Working above the Controllers were Managers who helped Gemini staff to keep control of the various aspects of the job. They too were not left out of the treats. There was a staff and managers' night out to somewhere that was fun, and they were allowed to bring their wives/husbands along who had, after all, been grass widows while Wimbledon was in progress. There was also a cocktail party for Managers and Controllers (no wives or husbands) at our offices around Christmas time. This was appreciated, as it was a get-together halfway between one Wimbledon and the next.

These methods kept us ticking over as a team and we were able to call on the services of the Wimbledon controllers and drivers to work on some of our other jobs too.

Of course not all the drivers were asked to come back the following year and the stories of some of them became legends with the team.

One driver who had been with us for a long time was frankly getting on in too many years to put him in the cars which would be under the scrutiny of the Press. He also began to wear really thick spectacles. We decided to relegate him to a less prominent but no less important role. So we put him on to driving the Junior tennis players' bus.

The Juniors were invited to Wimbledon as the top players of their country and came from tennis clubs all over the world. The Club also paid their expenses for the second week of the main tournament, when the Junior tournament took place. This was a great thrill for them and many took the opportunity to enter the senior competition and sometimes came successfully through it, such as John McEnroe and Bjorn Borg and many other famous names.

All seemed to be going well until our Juniors' Controller, Jenny Stanbrook, decided to hitch a lift on the Juniors' bus. She said she was surprised at how quiet the passengers appeared to be, particularly as the Juniors were not usually subdued. As they started the journey she observed that the driver was leaning forward in his seat and was tailgating the cars in front. She thought that perhaps his eyesight needed checking before he drove again, and she made a mental note to tell either Robin or me so we could take action.

The bus had a two-way radio on board and the aerial on this one became loose during the journey. The driver pulled in to a garage forecourt in order to fix it back on properly, which he did. They set off again, but instead of the driver exiting on the slip road, he mistakenly drove through the car wash. There was silence in the bus and Jenny at this point assumed he was either mad or couldn't see at all. She asked him to pull over and she took the wheel herself. We could not understand this. The driver had passed his driving test with us (or so we thought, later to learn he had slipped through the net); he had never had an accident and had held a clean driver's licence for many years. We told him he could not drive again until he had had his eyes re-tested and had taken some further driving tests. Those Junior players are probably still confused as to why the English exit through the car wash instead of the quicker slip road.

Before we had radios in the cars, and before mobile phones were in general use, another driver who was not to be invited back was asked to collect two players who had been practising at Queens' Club, Barons Court and bring them into Wimbledon.

The story goes he was late collecting them from Queens', and was then unsure of the way back to Wimbledon. He did however know the way to Heathrow Airport, and from there back to Wimbledon. So he decided to take this route.

Off they went to Heathrow. The two players did not speak much English and had no idea where they were, so they kept quiet. The driver, knowing he was running really late became flustered and when they arrived finally at Heathrow he couldn't remember the way back. He stopped a passing taxi and asked the driver how to get to Wimbledon. "Follow me," said the taxi driver, "I'm going into central London." As they were crossing Hammersmith Bridge unfortunately a Porsche car got between the taxi and the courtesy car. Our driver panicked and went too close to the Porsche and hit him in the rear.

The first I heard of this sorry tale was when a taxi driver arrived in my office in Wimbledon and asked me for £35 fare as he had led my courtesy car back. I also had a very irate pair of tennis players on my hands, threatening to complain about us, as they were late for their Wimbledon practice court booking. Then even worse, a really angry Porsche driver arrived, this was a promotional job with lots of money involved, demanded compensation for whiplash. He said his car was badly damaged and he wanted our insurance details. Well no, this driver was not invited back to Wimbledon the following year (he was lucky to be alive!) but yes; he did have the cheek to apply the following year.

Another driver who did come back, if only for his cheek was one Nadeem. He was lucky enough to pick up the tab for

Michael Stich, when Michael had won the Men's Singles Final at Wimbledon in 1991. As the courtesy car carrying Michael home after his win rounded the corner to his house, there were masses of Press people camped at his garden gate and in the road outside.

Michael, who was not used to this amount of attention, asked Nadeem to turn the car round and leave the area. Nadeem had the idea that they could go and have tea with his mother until the Press got tired of waiting, but he failed to let us know what was happening. I suspect he was afraid we might spoil his plans to have the Wimbledon Champion in his home on the night he won.

Alan Mills called me and asked had I seen Michael, and when I said yes, he had gone home in one of the courtesy cars, Alan asked me if the car could bring him back as he was needed for a Press conference on site. This did not appear to be a problem, so we sent a car to Michael's house to pick him up again, thinking that Nadeem must have dropped him off by now and was on his way back to Wimbledon empty.

We did not have two-way radios or mobiles at that time. The second car called in and said that Michael had never arrived at the house and the Press was beginning to disperse. Alan and I were both now worried that there had been an accident of some kind. Then Nadeem showed up, having finally dropped off Michael at his own house, as the Press had by this time left. Another car went to Michael's house and collected him for his on-site interview. Later that year I received a photograph of Michael and Nadeem taken outside Nadeem's home by Nadeem's proud mum, and on the back was written:

To Pat.

Just a reminder! One of my best days of Wimbledon '91. Michael outside my home having just won the Men's Singles title. I can hardly wait for next year's tournament!

Yours thankfully, Nadeem.

A driver who nearly drove my co-director Robin Webb potty was called Peter. Peter was a nice enough fellow but not the sharpest knife in the box. During training, it was stressed that the drivers must check their cars inside and out, every day, for security reasons. We were living in interesting times and we produced mirrors for checking the underneath of the cars. We pointed out that cars were a very easy target for bombers and that our drivers should be very aware for both their own and their passengers' safety.

Peter must have listened intently to the whole lecture. We were careful, however, not to make the drivers feel afraid of what might happen, because we had been in that position before. When we did the G7 summit in 1991, MI5 had given a lecture to the drivers about what happened when bombs went off. They backed up their lecture with horrific pictures which frightened the life out of the drivers, especially the girls, two of whom walked out and refused to work on the event. So we kept it very low key.

However, Peter decided to be extra vigilant, and every day he actually got under his car to look for bombs. We had fitted two-way radios that particular year, and there was some surplus wiring showing under the car. Peter became convinced the car was wired for a bomb, and every day he called poor Robin out to check the car.

By the end of the week, because he was spending so much time on the ground of the car park under his car, Peter was wearing a very dirty uniform shirt. I asked him to wear the second shirt we had provided for him and he replied that he couldn't, as it was one shirt for one week and one for the other. Why we had provided the drivers with non-iron drip-dry shirts I will never know.

We also had a cook who thought what we said might happen, would happen, and she became so obsessed about keeping her hands clean while handling the food that she washed her hands every time she made a sandwich. As there were around 400 sandwiches to make during the day, this could not go on. When I then told her to wash her hands only between handling meat and salads, I think she thought I wanted to poison everyone. As they say, "There's nowt so queer as folk."

There were other misdemeanours at The Championships, either committed by drivers or driver and players combined. One that springs to mind was early on in my days at Wimbledon when a lady driver came back to base, fuming in rage. "I really think it is disgraceful," she opined, "when a player and his girlfriend, and one of our ex-drivers at that, lie on the back seat of my car, with their feet sticking out of the open window, doing goodness-knows-what. It is embarrassing and what will the passers-by think." I asked to see the player and remonstrated with him. "We were just having a cuddle," he said. "Well not in my cars, you don't," I replied, testily. As far as I know that was the end of it.

Another player was very sweet on one of the very pretty girls who worked for me. They decided to buck the system when the player was leaving for the night and the driver's shift was finishing, so they could spend the rest of evening (night?) together.

The girl would collect her car keys for her last run as requested by our Controller, but instead of going to the player's exit she would drive behind the Covered Courts and meet up with the player there. The following morning, when she reported for duty, she would spike her journey ticket in the usual way. I don't think the drivers ever expected us to read the journey tickets but both Robin and I did. I smelled a rat, and one rainy night as she waited for the player to arrive, I walked to the back of the building and slid into her car instead. "Not expecting me were you?" I asked. "I know who you are waiting for and I will wait here with you until he arrives." And I did. I happened to know the player well and I knew he was engaged to another girl who was not travelling with him. He was very ashamed of himself and did not use the courtesy transport for about three more years, although he was perfectly entitled to. It was not until I bumped into him and told him he was very welcome to use it that he came back to us. He is now happily married and I am very happy he is so settled.

I used to warn the girl drivers that these young men have the world at their feet and a girl in every port (or should I say court), and I didn't want my drivers to get hurt if a player showed interest in them, but a lot of them did just that.

There are times when drivers can cause embarrassing moments. One I recall, which still makes me blush, was when I was trying to distribute sweaters for the male drivers to wear if it got cold in the late evenings. The sweaters were delivered in boxes and sized Small, Medium and Large. The drivers decided to help themselves to what they thought their size should be. They got all the sizes mixed up and chaos reigned. I took hold of the situation and made them return the sweaters to the correct boxes. "Put everything back and we will start again," I bellowed. "Now, step forwards anyone who has a big one." To a man the entire room stepped forward. After that I left the distribution to my assistants.

One of my lady Controllers in the early days started to see a very nice player to whom she lost her heart. As luck would have it he was also seeing one of my drivers. One day the Controller came into my office in floods of tears, and also in anger. She banged my desk and screamed and shouted and became hysterical. Once we had calmed her down she told us that she had found out about the player's interest in another girl and she was furious because the other girl was "only a driver". I could scarcely believe she had said that. The other girl was very sadly killed in a motor accident not long afterwards, when a lorry shed its load on her car. The Controller married another man. The tennis player, who had said to me on the day "You can't win them all, or even have them all." ("No," I replied, "but God loves a trier.") attended her wedding.

One lady driver took her car through the car wash and did not close the sunroof. When she returned to the office all she could say was could she go home and dry her hair as it was wet. As the car had to be returned to the factory and have brand new seats fitted it was a costly operation caused by her idiocy. "Of course you may" I said through gritted teeth "and do me a favour, don't come back again!" Mostly I hated having to get rid of people, but on some occasions it was a pleasure.

One time when my husband and I were visiting New York we were kindly invited to a party in a magnificent apartment on Park Avenue given by Cheeky Woolworth. There were a lot of tennis people there as the Americans have a special affinity with the sport, and welcome players and the rest of those involved to their homes. A very pretty girl came up to me and said, "You are Pat aren't you, from Wimbledon"? "Yes," I said, at a loss to know who she was. "I'm Andrea Jaeger," she said. "Oh," I said, "I remember you, you used to sit on the floor of my office blowing bubble gum and reading comics." "Please don't say that too loud," she said, and I did notice that there were quite a few young men looking her over at the time.

I didn't mention her past when she was the youngest player on the circuit and I always felt she was dumped on us to look after. When she played, of course, it was a different matter. Andrea now works very hard for charity, among other things, and she has changed from an ugly duckling to a swan, which is quite amazing. I have the greatest admiration for what she has achieved.

Janet Fenton was not the only one who was creative on the team. Several others, cartoonists, poets, and comedians were also included. Below are some extracts of their talents.

On the 21st year of my employment on The Championships I received a big card, signed by all the drivers and the verse inside, written by one of the drivers went as follows:

> "There is a lady, not afraid,
> To tell you where to go,
> She steers her teams with confidence,
> They're driven, not fast, not slow,
> Toe the line, you'll stay her friend,
> Skive and you will loathe her,
> Bend the rules, your luck may end,
> But NEVER bend her Rover."

(Written by a driver called Adrian)

Part of another poem, written by Nigel Ford after a "Midweek" BBC Radio 4 Interview which I did at the Club's request went:

> "Wimbledon players and 'chauffeurettes'
> There's nothing ahead but troubles
> From those who are driven to their hotels
> And want to play mixed doubles.

> But Patricia Banks is smiling still,
> *(This was written before I married Ian Edwards)*
> Despite the thought of stars,
> Who having failed to break service,
> Attempt to break up her cars."

Chapter 4

THE COMMITTEE

People are often curious about how Wimbledon actually operates and what happens there for the other fifty weeks of the year.

The All England Club that runs The Championships in June is a private tennis club and has 360 full members plus a number of temporary and honorary members. From these members, and voted by these members, a Committee of Management is elected to run the Club's affairs.

This committee does not run The Championships, but the same Club Committee members, when joined by the Lawn Tennis Association Committee form the Committee of Management of The Championships. This is because the Wimbledon tournament can only run with the approval of the LTA as the ruling body of the game in the UK. There is some juxtaposition to get places on the Club Committee, where some members who have retired from their full-time careers can shine again in the large multi-national business that Wimbledon has become.

There are also six executive directors, led by the Chief Executive, a post held by Chris Gorringe until 2005. In addition the Club Secretary is closely involved with the executive team, though his responsibility is the running of the Club as a tennis club in its own right and to look after the tennis club members. The duties of the executive are, Championships Director, a post held by Richard Grier, Finance Director, Tony Hughes (due to retire I believe in 2007); Marketing Director, Rob McCowen;

Director of Television, J. Rowlinson; IT Director, Jeff Lucas.

Below the executive are the middle managers, who deal with the co-ordination of the Championships, these include the Ticket Manager (a crucial role), The Championships Coordinator, the Buildings and Services Manager, and the Head Groundsman – all of whom have their own departments employing all year round staff. Then there are the permanent secretaries and assistants to the executive and the managers, the receptionists, and the permanent catering staff.

In 1972 there was only a staff of one Club Secretary, who organised both the tournament and the club members. He had an assistant, who was Tony Cooper when I first worked there, two secretaries, the groundsman and his staff, a few maintenance men and a small catering department which consisted of a husband and wife team. The number of temporary staff has swelled to several thousand from only a few, without whose contribution The Championships could not run. These include security, catering, stewards (military and honorary, who have been there since 1972 although not in such large numbers), transport, media – both written press and television, not forgetting Radio Wimbledon which opened in 1992 – match officials, referees, court coverers, and score board operatives, and of course the ball boys (and girls since 1977).

When I began to work at Wimbledon there was a lady called Lottie who did the in-house catering for the then small number of staff and members. She ruled the roost and the members were certainly under her thumb, but her jam tarts were to die for! Her husband Leo was the small man who could be seen on television staggering under the weight of the enormous bags he carried for the strapping singles players onto Centre Court for the finals matches. These two were real characters, famous in their own right within tennis circles and they helped give Wimbledon that feeling of family that it used to have but which now I fear has gone forever.

A lot of this growth was due to the swashbuckling agent, Mark McCormack, one of the most powerful people in sport. In the beginning I used to tease him and say he was a ten-per-center. As he and Wimbledon grew in stature and he persuaded the Club and the Championships Committee to change and develop Wimbledon into the incredible multi-million-pound empire it is today, that nickname had to go.

Mark himself did not change with the years. He was still kind and considerate, ready with advice and encouragement. Once when I had been fighting hard with the Club to get the salaries of my drivers to a higher level I was surprised when Mark accosted me on the Royal Steps. "Did you get what you wanted?" Mark shouted. I left my husband who was with me at the time and walked over to Mark. "Yes," I said. "Great," he replied, and we did high fives together. My husband was very amused to watch this performance.

I remember the incident when I was a recipient of Mark's kindness. It was Mark's generous custom to entertain the executive for a special evening before each Championship began. He usually gave a dinner at Hampton Court Palace, while his company IMG sponsored the annual Music Festival and to which each of his dinner guests were invited after Mark's dinner party.

This particular night once fell on my birthday. I was delighted to have been invited to the party and been looking forward to it all week. The dinner was held in Hampton Court's Banqueting House and the dinner table was breathtaking with the flowers in purple and green and the silver candlesticks spreading candlelight over the beautiful old building.

Mark stood up to make his welcome speech to everyone. He opened it with something along the lines: "You may all think this dinner is to celebrate the start of The Championships. The dinner tonight, however, is in honour of our Birthday Girl." I don't know who told him it was my birthday, although I suspect it was Chris Gorringe who never forgets those special occasions. However it made a very memorable night for me, especially as Mark took a photograph of me that night at the table and sent me a copy with a sweet note attached which I will always keep. Like a lot of people I was devastated by his death in 2003.

Some of the people who served on the committee in my early days at The Club deserve a mention. In 1972 the committee members were of the old school and they knew how to behave like gentlemen. They were known however as 'the Blimps', a shortened form of Colonel Blimp, as they were seen as being a bit stuffy and the Club was dominated at that time by the military.

There are many moments I will never forget. One morning I was summoned to a Press Meeting during the championships where Roy McKelvie the Press Officer and his helper Bill Edwards, both sports journalists in real life, were ranting on about how they felt a situation should be dealt with. This argument went backwards and forwards between them for some time. I was busy at the time and got quickly to the end of my patience and said, completely out of turn, "You are both talking bullshit." There was complete silence. The old committee member sitting to my left rounded on me with a look of complete horror on his face. "Oh I say, old girl," he said, "have another sherry." My annoyance evaporated instantly and I had great difficulty in keeping a straight face as I apologised for my language.

On another occasion, when one of my team had had to refuse John Austin, brother of Tracy Austin, a favour which was not allowed by the Club, he tore into my office, dragged me off my chair and slammed me against the wall with his hand round my throat. I am 5' 6" and he at a guess is around 6' 0" and very strong, as most of the tennis players are. I was terrified, especially as I didn't know why he was attacking me.

Into the office rushed Ted Avory, an old club and committee

member who had been a well-known tennis player in his time. He saw what was happening, grabbed John's arm and said, "I say, Sir, you are a cad, unhand her at once." John, surprised, dropped me like a hot brick and I slithered down the wall, teeth chattering, to the floor, shocked but otherwise unharmed.

Ted fussed around and proceeded to administer the Club's recipe for all ills, an eye-crossing G & T. John came back later to my office with his grandparents who were at Wimbledon to watch him and Tracy play. He apologised profusely and said he did not know what had come over him. It was just one of those moments when you lose control and see red. The tennis players were all very highly tensed up and John thought I made the Club rules. Tennis players can be dumb sometimes.

Another of my favourite people in those days was Stanley Hawkins. Stanley I believe was the first person to get a gong from the Queen for services to tennis and he was justly proud of it and of his position at Wimbledon. At the time Stanley was around, my secretary and I used to receive a nice lunch on a tray which was delivered to our office each day of the tournament. Sadly this custom was dropped later when we hired a sandwich maker for the drivers; we had the same thing as I didn't feel I could have more than the people who worked for me. It certainly was my loss.

However, Stanley ate his lunch later than ours was delivered but even so he still called into my office to take me to lunch at the Members Enclosure. This is a privileged area that is open only to members of the Club and their families and friends. Every day Stanley would have smoked salmon and brown bread and butter accompanied by some very large gin and tonics. As I had usually eaten I just had the gin and tonic, in smaller quantities I might add, but it still made me wavery in the afternoon.

Stanley always chatted up the waitress from Town and County who had orange hair and looked like an escapee from the Music Hall. She must have been well into her eighties but this did not deter Stanley. At that time Town and County did the catering for The Championships over the fortnight and Lottie did the catering for the Club staff for the rest of the year. An Air Vice Marshal with a death wish, who was in charge of catering as his committee job, had unfortunately signed a very long 22-year contract with these caterers. Armed with this contract it was not unusual for Town and County to run out of the strawberry cream teas and to serve digestive biscuits instead. Somehow I believe the Club managed to renegotiate the contract.

The caterers Town and County stayed on for a while afterwards, only to reorganise themselves as another company towards the end of the century. These days the catering is very much improved, although working at Wimbledon tended to put me off strawberries for good.

In 1972 the Secretary of The Club was H.F. David C.B.E. This changed in 1974 to Air Chief Marshal Sir Brian K Burnett. Both of these Chairman ran the Club in a very military fashion. Sir Brian was of the old school and a stickler for good behaviour. Thankfully my transport department satisfied him as we made sure we were always early to collect him but kept the car out of site of his house until the absolute minute he had asked for it.

He was always very admiring of punctuality. He was not so admiring of John McEnroe. I can still see the look on Sir Brian's face as he stood on the Royal Steps on the first morning of The Championships to welcome players in. As John arrived he whistled past Sir Brian, oblivious as to his presence, on roller blades with his earphones plugged in listening to music. The look of bewilderment on Sir Brian's face showed that things were beginning to change at SW19 – arguably not always for the better.

The Chairman who followed Sir Brian was Buzzer

Hadingham, someone I had known socially for some time before I came to Wimbledon. Buzzer was a handsome, dapper man, with a great deal of charm. He always struck me as the type of person who could easily have fitted in as a character in a Noel Coward play. He was extremely good at handling people, the Press in particular.

Buzzer liked to tell a joke if he was speaking after dinner. The jokes could be quite funny the first time round but he had a habit of repeating them at each dinner he went to in a single year and that could be quite trying. He always said after the toasts were over, "If you must, you may" although he was not a smoker himself which I found rather endearing.

The next chairman was John Curry who took office in 1989. John is a larger than life character, hugely dynamic, and I speak from experience. He had also won an Oxford rugby blue as a prop forward so the size matched the personality. Before John was appointed Chairman of The All England Club he had been Chairman of our transport sub-committee.

During his time with transport he and I had heated arguments over a variety of transport matters. We banged the table and shouted a good deal but I like to think we will always remain friends. He was also a powerful and successful business man but he was not too grand to 'roll his sleeves up' when the occasion arose.

Once when it was raining hard in the evening, play had been cancelled and everyone at The Championships that day wanted to get home. When everyone leaves at once the roads get jammed, the cars do not get back in time to make the usual couple of journeys and we run out of vehicles for an hour or so. It was one of those evenings.

John came over to transport HQ in Somerset Road to see how we were getting on. He could see our dilemma. "What can I do to help?" he asked after I had explained the situation. "The only thing I need now is drivers and cars," I replied. "OK," he said, "here I am, with my car, tell me what to do." I took him at his word and gratefully bundled four fretful tennis players on board and off John drove, with a map and a smile. He was gone for ages and afterwards laughingly admitted he had got a bit lost on the way.

Later that year it was announced that John had been appointed as the new Chairman of The All England Club. I wrote him a letter of congratulations on his appointment, adding as a postscript 'I hope you make a better Chairman than you did a driver'. He actually made a brilliant chairman and remained to run the Club for ten years. Everyone was sorry to see him leave and he was persuaded to stay on longer than his time as he had been so effective.

With John running the whole shooting match, the transport sub-committee needed a new chairman. Richard Grier called me to say The Lord Kindersley had been appointed. Lord Kindersley is nothing like John Curry; the only thing they possibly have in common is that they both studied at The Harvard School of Business in the States. Lord Kindersley looks as a Lord should look. He is tall, slim with fair hair and a pale skin. On first impressions he appears to have a diffident manner and he is extremely polite. I was a little dismayed because I was used to John's manner which is forceful and definite.

My first brush with Hugo Kindersley was when he decided to check out how my staff and I actually ran the transport operation at Wimbledon. I was outraged. I felt that if they didn't like what I was doing they were a bit late in telling me after eighteen years of service. Lord Kindersley insisted, in a quiet manner, that we should be checked out and the P.A. Consulting Group were engaged to do just that. It was not pleasant to have people with you all the time you worked, noting everything down as you went through your day.

When P.A. finally said they were ready to report we were apprehensive. My secretary and I had helped them to write out a plan of how we did everything. I was surprised when the Club took the plan and used it as the basis of their Management Plan which merely told us to do what we had told P.A. we did in the first place.

Even though I had taken out a copyright on the book form of my service, I agreed to this. This plan which was to become the Club's Management Plan was still being used by them to the day I left. I felt that the £30,000 the Club spent on this venture could have been spent on the transport operation which really needed roads about the grounds strengthening to take the weight of the buses we were now using for the Public Park and Ride service.

P.A. reported that we were doing a good job and they recommended two very small changes that were easily incorporated into our daily lives. They also said we did not charge enough for our services which enabled us to put our fees up. I began to change my mind about Lord Hugo Kindersley. As time went on I got to know him better and his attractive wife Tita. I finished employing his stepdaughter Theresa as my PA. She turned out to be one of the best I ever had.

Surprisingly Hugo loved to sing and perform in front of an audience. At our driver briefings each year he used to prepare poems and songs to perform, which were usually dedicated to me. The drivers really liked this part of the proceedings and Hugo was excellent at managing them in this way. They all liked him and found him good fun and went out of their way to make things happen even when the task he set was almost impossible.

I am not sure that these skills had been learned at Harvard but he certainly was a good man manager. His signature tune was 'Here we are again, happy as can be, all good pals and jolly good company'. This was also adopted by the drivers and sung when he entered the room.

Sometimes Hugo was a little hard to find when I needed him

to make a decision. In desperation one day when he had disappeared for the umpteenth time I wrote a poem to him which I put in the internal mail, hoping someone would know where he was. It went as follows-

They seek him here, they seek him there,
Transport seeks him everywhere.
Is he on court, or gone for tea?
That dammed elusive Kindersley.

He appeared in transport regularly after that.

The Referees' Office

Since joining Wimbledon in 1972 there have also been several changes in the Referee's office. When I joined, Captain Mike Gibson was officiating. Mike was quite the ladies' man and some hushed-up scandals about him were the gossip of the day. A handsome man, who attracted the attention of some of my lady drivers, as much as the tennis players did. Holding romances back was quite a task generally.

When Mike left, reluctantly I believe, he handed the referee's reins to Fred Hoyles. Fred was a bachelor farmer who lived with his two sisters in Lincolnshire and usually stayed in lodgings near Wimbledon where we collected him in the morning. Referees, and assistant referees, were allowed courtesy cars because their days are so long and difficult.

The only trouble the transport department had with Fred and the lady drivers was not romance but the fact that Fred was, for some reason, irritated by them and often made them cry. On one occasion he complained his driver was one minute late, which I had words with him about. However he was a good referee and well thought of by his office staff of 15, although we were quite glad when in 1983 he decided to retire after a spat on court with John McEnroe.

In 1983 Alan Mills, who had been Fred's assistant, took over and I was very relieved. I had met Alan many years previously in Liverpool which was our home town. I had watched him play tennis as a young man many times when I attended the Lancashire Championships with my tennis player boyfriend, Dave Abram. I knew that Alan was a calm and steady person and would be a good influence at Wimbledon. I like to think that our two departments worked closely together and I hope that we gave the referee's office, as well as Alan, Tony Gathercole, Jean Sexton and the rest a good service. We certainly enjoyed their company and had a lot of fun with them.

When John Curry was Chairman of The Club he wandered over to the covered courts where the transport department was housed and asked one of my traffic controllers for a car. The controller asked for John's name. "Don't you know who I am?" boomed John. "No Sir," was the reply. "Do you know who the Chairman of the All England Club is?" asked John. "Oh yes, Sir," the controller replied, "It's Alan Mills."

I don't think we employed that controller again, although Alan Mills was very chuffed.

Chapter 5

THE TRANSPORT SERVICE

Setting out for a day at Wimbledon, the first thing a passenger sees in the morning is their courtesy car. The last thing they see at night is their courtesy car. No matter how the day has progressed for them in between these two events, it is the impression that the transport service gives that sets the mood and the perception of that passenger as to how efficient Wimbledon is. Thus a transport service is of the utmost importance to any event and must be run efficiently and professionally.

To say a workman always blames his tools is nonsense. If your hammer breaks you can't knock the nail in. If your facilities and accommodations are bad then your work will suffer. I have worked on many diverse events, including Wimbledon, the Olympics, and London Fashion Week to name but a few, but on all of them, without exception, the transport service they are running is always the last service to be considered.

For years at Wimbledon we requested larger premises because the facilities given to us were unsuitable. The local council actually condemned our offices up to the year 2000. Due to the size of the operation there were never enough seats in the 'crew' room for the drivers to sit down and rest between runs.

The kitchen improved but only because the local health authority demanded that the club bring it up to the legal standards

Engraving the plate.

Two members of the press in AELT
idea of a Press Office for Transport

The Armed Forces entertaining at a rainy Wimbledon.

required. When the year 2000 arrived and the new building opened for players and staff, my office was so small I could not get even one of the smaller desks into it. It is now used to hang coats in. No matter which country I have visited to advise on sports events, it is always the same disappointing story.

"Let the drivers sit in their cars," stated one fat member of the Wimbledon Committee of Management in 1999 when I requested at a meeting to discuss appropriate seating for everyone in their 'crew' room. This was just what the drivers had to do in 1972 and this was 27 years later. So much for moving forward.

When I left in 2004 we were still short of adequate seating. The temporary nature of the job means that drivers are not chauffeurs as such, but merely doing a very short temporary job. To leave them sitting in their cars all day, waiting to be sent out, would cause no end of problems – that is, if they agreed to do the job at all under such circumstances. After all, the £7.50 per hour which the Club agreed they should be paid amounted to very little on the open market, in fact my cleaner earns more than that and she does not have the responsibility or pressure that these drivers have to work under.

We tried to run an efficient operation despite tube strikes, rain, road works, burst water mains, overloaded guest lists, the excessive demands of players, the tricky location of Wimbledon in relation to central London, the extra traffic which descended on the small streets around the grounds during the tournament, and numerous other irritations. We did, however, run an efficient transport service and we were congratulated over the years as being the best of its type in the world.

The success of the service was due to the planning beforehand. We were fortunate that Wimbledon was an annual event. However the demands of the occasion grew each time, and it was never the same year on year.

There were several watersheds along the way. In 1972 British Leyland supplied the cars and paid the drivers' salaries. At that time, the Club realised there was a positive change in their transport arrangements, and they took full advantage of the 50 cars and girl drivers. According to British Leyland's records, 300 people used the service that year. Training days for drivers were held on the weekend before The Championships began. The 8 hours working time for the drivers was broken into two halves with a break in the afternoon, this following the Club's request that players and a couple of officials should be brought into the grounds between 10 a.m. and 1 p.m., and taken home between 5 p.m. and 9 p.m. Any overtime after 9 p.m. was paid at the same rate. Play in those days began at 2 p.m. in order that the Club members could enjoy their lunch, and there was no play on Sundays. Players also needed to practise from 10 a.m. at Queens Club in west London.

It is stated in the 1972 report that "the parking facilities offered by the committee was extremely inadequate and caused considerable difficulties for the operations staff. The 'holding area' was too far away, causing delays in reaching the waiting passengers due to the crowds and one-way systems." Also on this theme it appeared that the two-way radio we had been supplied with kept breaking up and could not be used because of interference from police walkie-talkies.

The field telephone connected to the holding area was also inadequate, working only intermittently, and when it did ring, a stranger who happened to be passing by the tree that it was hanging from often answered it. There was optimism that all this would change by the following year, and we felt that this incompetence could only be down to teething troubles in the first year.

After the 1973 Championships we were still using the outlying parking area, the field telephone was still not working properly and the walkie-talkies had been put to one side. British Leyland's report said "It was also noted that the space for Club

Members' cars was not fully used by them and was being allocated by the AA (Automobile Association) to members of the public. Could this not have been made available to us this year?" I recall that George Holmes took this up with the AA, who said they were not charging for the spaces.

We also requested a caravan with tea and coffee-making facilities for the girl drivers, who were advised to bring their own packed lunches with them, in view of the prohibitively high price of refreshment within the Wimbledon grounds. We also asked for a small minibus to be added to the fleet, because the passenger list appeared to have risen to 350.

1974 saw a new rest area for the drivers and, wonder of wonders, a colour television. We also took the liberty of asking for a hot meal for the drivers! Lunch and tea tickets had been provided for the final Sunday in that year, which was in those days extended play as Wimbledon normally finished on the final Saturday. We wondered why could this not be done every day. Apparently we received a Royal accolade this year, for driving a member of the Royal Family and her staff in one of the Morris Marinas we were using at that time.

In 1974 a letter from George Holmes to Major Mills, then Secretary and Treasurer to the Club, states that there would be a change of vehicle to a larger model. He also requested running an 11-seater coach from Queens Club, the players' practice area, to Wimbledon. This was because individual Club staff at Queens kept telephoning for a car for their own use, instead of maximising the available seats in other cars. On one occasion they apparently ordered eight cars in one hour, which caused a shortage of vehicles at the Wimbledon end. We came to refer to this as our Shuttle Service.

By now, Committee members were also jumping onto the bandwagon. They were coming into Wimbledon early, and then insisting on sending the same car back home to collect their wives. George refused to do this because we were so short of cars. We were also requesting a limitation on the number of people using the cars and requesting lists from the Club as to who could travel. George asked that the Club should give ten more match tickets to British Leyland, to make up for these inconveniences.

In 1977 there was a meeting attended by Gerry Williams (broadcaster), Bill Edwards (Tennis Writers' Association), Mike Lee of British Leyland (unfortunately George Holmes had moved over into another position in British Leyland) and Pat Edwards and Annie Dickins of Promcat Ltd., which was the name of my company at the time. The upshot was that Leyland agreed to add three more cars to the Wimbledon fleet.

In Gerry Williams's letter to David Mills, he stated that the transport facilities for the Press were inadequate and that one of the purposes of the meeting was to provide goodwill to foreign journalists and provincial sports writers, basing themselves in London for the Fortnight (the Press in fact were not at that time entitled to any transport at all, and kept attacking Annie and me about it, sometimes with considerable aggravation). It was agreed that 100 passes should be printed and handed out by Bill Edwards, on request, for a Press journey. The service was to run from the Gloucester Hotel, Earls Court, and Wimbledon. However, the limitations were quickly forgotten when the passes were handed out and 100 were given on the first day. We had only three cars to provide this service. By 2004, we had as many as 12 Press buses and 24 drivers.

In 1978 I was still requesting hot food for the drivers, better means of communicating other than the field telephone, and better accommodation for the staff. This year was also to see the beginning of a major change in the volume of the service. The number of people travelling in the morning had risen to 400, and those travelling home had risen to 500. We had no explanation for this large difference. We knew some people travelled in from practice courts by using London Underground trains, and got a lift home from us in the evening. We therefore expected the night list to be bigger, but certainly not by as much as 100.

Insurance was discovered to be inadequate after an accident in 1977 involving a lady driver who was hit by a Barkers of Kensington lorry, and who could not return to her normal job because of her injuries. Most car companies only insured their cars for third party, fire and theft, as did British Leyland, which was quite adequate. However, this basic insurance does not cover the driver if they cause the accident. This lady was not to blame for this accident, so she was covered, but the team was not covered for an accident if one of the drivers had caused it. After lengthy discussions, the Club came up trumps and took out a personal accident policy on the entire driving team, which amounted to better insurance coverage than if the policy had been fully comprehensive. This came as a great relief.

We were now bringing in and taking home some top Wimbledon operational staff such as the Referee and his two assistants, and this entailed very late nights. This was because after play finished, the following day's Order of Play had to be worked on. After this, the officials went into the Club for supper and then needed to be driven home.

My controllers and I did not leave until there were no more passengers on site, so we needed to be taken home too. This meant a switchover of shifts to accommodate these extra requirements.

Main service time: 10.30 a.m. – 2.15 p.m.
                       5.15 p.m. – 12 midnight
Officials' service time: 8.00 a.m. – 12 midnight

There was a small skeleton staff employed from 9 a.m. to 5 p.m. to deal with stragglers, emergencies etc.

We also had some problems with people abusing the system, involving players at Queens' Club getting into a car or bus from there to Wimbledon while their wives/husbands telephoned from their hotels in the same player's name, asking for another car, therefore tying up two vehicles at busy periods.

In the evening, passengers normally asked to go to their hotel, and this procedure was logged out on the Royal Steps, next to our then office. The passenger then often tended to browbeat the driver into taking them to a club, restaurant or theatre in Central London. This was done not only by the players but also by VIPs, and it was often difficult and unpleasant for the driver to refuse such requests.

Some players also asked for a car parking ticket in order to bring in their own car, and then ordered an official car on the day they were playing. Their coach and family would then use the parking ticket, tying up two vehicles.

These difficulties came to such a point that we requested the Club to write an official letter to all those entitled to use the service, in order to explain the rules. We felt we could not provide an efficient service until everyone knew where they stood. We didn't care who used the service, but we did care that those who were entitled to travel did so, and were not inconvenienced by other people's behaviour. Bad weather conditions in this year simply made things worse.

Nineteen-eighty was a watershed. This was one of the worst years, weather-wise, that we ever experienced. It was a year when the cars had to be towed out of the mud by the AA.

By now, 293 VIPs, together with their wives/husbands travelled in addition to the entire draw of tennis players. Junior players and members of the Press also had their own services in addition to the main transport services. However, we only had 57 cars. The problem was that all these people wished to travel around the same time. Had the time been spread out we could have managed it better.

I realised that the schedules needed to be completely reworked, and that more drivers had to be employed the following year. In 1980 the 75 drivers worked 408 hours of overtime, and were exhausted. It worried me that to work them for so many hours was dangerous. My recommendations to the Club that year were as follows:

To alleviate some of the pressures and ensure a more efficient and safe service, it is recommended that: [and I quote] "A clear and concise letter is sent to every person using the service stating exactly what is available for their use and a copy of this letter should be displayed in the transport offices.

Complete lists of officials who have received the above letter should be given to transport the week before Wimbledon, so we can plan ahead.

Players are allowed one guest on the day they are competing only. This would allow transport to calculate numbers the evening before. Different coloured tickets would be given to players on the day they were competing. When a player is out of the tournament they are no longer eligible to travel.

Officials and press should have a limited number of seats available – limits to be sensibly agreed upon.

Driver's welfare should be put more to the fore in pre-planning stages.

Better housing facilities for this growing service should be explored.

Transport should be allowed to refuse to provide extra facilities such as coping with lost property, minding luggage, accepting rackets for stringing etc.

A return to 50 cars and 2 buses is recommended, the buses merely to be used on a sweeper service.

A list of people eligible to travel in the courtesy cars to the LTA Ball and Savoy dinner should be given to Transport in the week preceding Wimbledon. The people on that list should be asked to give Transport two days' advance notice if they actually do require a car on either of the two evenings, otherwise Transport will not be able to make a car available (Of course this rule does not include the Chairman!)."

Well that was telling them but did it all happen? What do you think?

The following year, 831 passengers were moved in the morning and 909 were transported in the evening. The cars in those days could make around three journeys in the morning, and about four in the evening as the cars could be packed more easily. We also discovered this year that some LTA and All England Club Secretarial Staff were travelling, which we requested should be cut out altogether. We also suggested that the lists should be limited to players and 100 other passengers only. In addition, we requested 45 cars and 4 minibuses so that we could do bulk carrying from the hotels. Our transport office, which only had room for two people at times during the day, was housing seven. However, the drivers did have the use of a marquee by the old covered courts, and this was appreciated.

By now our driving team had risen to 89. The drivers were also able to apply for 12 Wimbledon tickets for Number 1 Court. These were for seats mainly behind pillars, and could not be sold to the public at full price because of the impaired view of play. Still, the drivers were luckier than the crowds outside, and their badges also allowed them into the grounds to watch tennis on the outside courts. This was a privilege much appreciated by the drivers. The Club also agreed that in the following year we would be allowed to hand out travel tickets to all people travelling, other than competitors, who are entitled to transport.

Nineteen-eighty-two was the year when we all started to work for 13 days and The Championships ended on a Sunday. This year also saw a new service, the Airport Shuttle, springing up. We were given two minibuses to use on airport runs as an hourly shuttle between Heathrow and Wimbledon. Twenty-six of the 52 Austin Ambassador cars had two drivers to enable us to have longer shift times. This was because the Club had decided that the transport service should run throughout the afternoon as well.

Again we rescheduled. Three minibuses in addition to the airport ones were also used. This was really helpful as it was one of the wettest years on record, and we also suffered from the effects of a London Tube strike over the first eight days of The Championships.

The Referee had a dreadful job rescheduling matches, and we did our best to keep up with players who were going backwards and forwards between their digs and Wimbledon like yo-yos. A Veterans' Over 35 Invitation Singles was added to the tournament schedule and doubles events were added to the Junior Championships. This meant more and more people wanted transport.

At the end of the 1982 Championships, ten years after I had started to run the service, as many as a thousand people were being transported as opposed to the 300 passengers in 1972. The car numbers had increased by 2, although 7 minibuses were now added to the fleet. These were, however, covering two extra services that we had not been required to run in 1972.

We had also been requested to supply 10 cars and drivers during the week preceding Wimbledon, known initially as Overseas Week although this title changed to Practice Week when it covered all competitors in the main draw and not just the ones from overseas. We supplied the 10 cars with two drivers from the Wednesday of this week, but it proved to be inadequate. This was the week we normally used to train the drivers and set up our offices.

One of the things we did on these training days was to put a driver who had worked for us previously together with a new driver to learn the routes. The Club never learned to do things properly from the beginning, and we ended up having to put old drivers in separate cars to look after the players during Overseas Week as 10 cars was inadequate.

The Club persuaded British Leyland to expand the service a little more each year by adding more days, more people, and more events. Inevitably, the costs to British Leyland continued to rise. At the same time, they unfortunately cut down Leyland's annual ticket allocation and made them pay half the cost for their advertisement in the Wimbledon magazine, which had originally been free. Diana Tovey from British Leyland remonstrated about these changes but it did not appear to make any difference.

A great deal of money was now being spent on the transport service owing to the extra drivers and vehicles, and there seemed to be a feeling of discontent emanating from British Leyland. They were not getting much in the way of promotional advantages, and they were not allowed to use the name of the Club in the way that normal sponsorship allowed. The Club denied having any sponsorship at all, preferring to call it "official suppliers". Had George Holmes been left in charge this would never have been allowed to happen.

The weather had not been good in this year either, but now we did at least have a proper telephone system and better parking areas. We were still requesting proper food for the drivers, hot if possible, but our recommendation of a food van as used by film companies on location had come to naught. I felt that the conditions under which the drivers were working, due to the extra work and the appalling weather, were simply not good enough.

Because of these poor weather conditions, and increased numbers travelling, we had to bring the entire fleet of cars in one hour earlier. This whacked up the hours of overtime. After consulting the official Wimbledon doctor, who agreed that the hours and circumstances under which the drivers worked were dangerous, we suggested that two drivers should man all cars. This would keep the cars on the road for 16 hours a day.

No-one stuck to the previous year's request regarding the

LTA Ball or the Champions' Dinner, and people continued to call for cars to take them to these events in Central London half an hour before they needed them.

We suggested that there should be a separate press service with an adequate number of vehicles to cover their requests. We asked for the Club to give us the numbers of those whom they thought merited transport. All in all this was a most difficult and unpleasant year and I seriously doubted whether I would carry on working on the project.

1983. The provision of a full courtesy car service for the competitors for the nine practice days before The Championships starts at the practice venues and the qualifying competition. These extra days were not covered by the contract between the Club and British Leyland. Leyland stood its ground, and though it was happy to supply the vehicles it was not prepared to pay for the extra driving and supervisory team, nor for the extra insurance and petrol needed for extra drivers brought about by the ever-increasing requests from the Club to accommodate more passengers.

The Club wanted a full transport service from 8 a.m. till midnight plus all the extra days we were now working. The Club felt, according to one report, that Leyland should meet these costs in 1984 or it suggested Leyland reduce the amount of cars and add to the number of minibuses. It was never mentioned that the Club might consider cutting the number of people travelling. What good they felt this might do I will never know as this suggestion would not have worked because it lacked the flexibility we needed and I was glad to see Leyland squashed it flat. They did, however, offer an additional £5,000 over budget to help the Club out.

It was assumed that in 1984, due to the extra drivers, the transport service would be able to cope with the Ball and Champions' Dinner, whoever wished to travel. Of course the transport service was still running players about at the times when people wanted to go to the Ball. So we were not much better off. Picking up from the Ball at 2.30 a.m. was not a problem because all the cars could then be made available. So the mayhem went on, on those two nights.

We were also allowed to put our Controllers into the tournament hotels to run the minibus shuttle. This was working well except for those VIPs who refused to use the bus shuttle and we had to send cars to collect them instead. It was clearly a case of vanity and not convenience. Group outings were also being considered using the courtesy transport.

In 1984 a new problem arose. We had always used all the hard standing around the Covered Courts for the courtesy cars and the Royal Cars. Before the tournament started, the Royal Cars were absent so we trained the drivers over the hard standing without interference. The Club, however, decided this year to park all the staff cars on this area during the week before the tournament. This meant we had no space for the drivers' training days. To train them on the grounds away from the hard standing would have ploughed up the grass with the constant movement.

The Club also locked the public lavatories, which were based in the near vicinity of transport. This meant that the public began using the drivers' loos, often causing the drivers to queue, which made them late for pickups. We locked our private loos and the public broke the locks. We also did not receive our full consignment of uniform until the end of the first week of the tournament, so drivers were using their own clothes, which did not look terrific and it upset those drivers still waiting for their uniforms. Some of the junior players kept missing their bus home and coming to us for help.

The Club only took responsibility for junior players who stayed in the designated hotels, for which the Club paid the players an allowance. A bus service ran to these hotels which in those days was under the control of the Club staff.

However, we felt obliged to take care of those juniors who missed their last bus, usually because their matches had been rescheduled or they had taken too long in the shower, as we could not have young foreigners who did not know their way around our large city trying to get home on their own. It appeared that the lady member of the Club staff who looked after them did not wait until all the juniors were off the premises.

We suggested tentatively that a representative from my company should attend the meeting which discussed the Junior Players' trip to Wimbledon for the following year with a view to solving these problems if at all possible. All in all this year was not one of our most memorable. Had the Club sorted out some of these problems in advance, our job would have been a lot easier.

This was the year that Chris Gorringe became Chief Executive and the new posts of Club Secretary and Championships Director were created.

Nineteen-eighty-four saw the Centenary of the Ladies' Championship. This was celebrated on the second Monday of The Championships, and caused a whole lot of running about for transport as the former champions needed to book cars in time to parade on Centre Court. A ladies' military band played on the two finals days of this year.

Fred Perry was made much of by the Club and they unveiled a statue to commemorate his win at Wimbledon 50 years earlier. Fred loved the fuss but as always, being a grounded northerner, he said to me, "They didn't like me when I won it, so what's all the fuss about now?" Fred always made me laugh. He always wrote to thank me for all we had done for him and his wife Bobby.

After Fred died, Bobby wrote to me to say how she was getting on. I also have letters from Fred and from Kitty Godfree in my desk, which I treasure. This year, Sir Brian Burnett retired and I was sorry to see him go, although I was happy that my old friend Buzzer (Hadingham) succeeded him as Club Chairman.

The following year, 1985, the transport system for The Championships entered into a new five-year contract, with British Leyland now named Austin Rover. The new service provided 54 cars and 12 minibuses. 44 of these cars had two drivers on 8-hour shifts, giving a 16-hour a day vehicle usage. 10 cars had one driver each on a split shift to cover mainly peak periods.

The minibuses split into two groups of six. The first six were used on the same two-driver basis as the 44 cars, to provide maximum usage. The second set of six was on a split shift system to meet the time requirements specified by the Press committee for overseas journalists. Using the vehicles in this fashion was not the easiest way to run things but it was the most economical in order to help the situation.

During this year it rained heavily. As the practice area at Queens' Club was rained off, it was decided that the players should use the David Lloyd Club in Raynes Park for practice. The players appeared to be happy about this even though it was quite far out, making journey times longer from central London. Of course this caused a shortage of cars and the rain also conspired to delay journeys to the Club.

The number of people allowed to travel this year was more than 1,000 (not including the Press) as opposed to last year's 950. We were still dispatching people from the Royal Steps inside the grounds of Wimbledon, and as the amount of people travelling grew, the swell of the crowd of players and VIPs on the steps became almost impossible to control. We begged the Club again to prune its guest list, and I made my first suggestion that the visitors should be dispatched separately from the players, as the two factions were becoming alienated as they waited for their transport.

The AA had to lay corrugated sheeting over the ground for us to get out of the mud, and straight away the All England Club staff began to park on it, so that we could not use it. We were also having fun at the tournament hotels, which were not providing adequate parking spaces for us, even though we were bringing players as customers to the hotels. Players always preferred to book a hotel room where there was a transport desk so they could be sure of a ride out to Wimbledon.

After the previous year's driver uniform fiasco I asked the Club if I could take over the obtaining of these garments so I would make sure they arrived on time.

In 1985 the Club's executive staff was restructured with new posts being created for Championships Director, Financial Director, Marketing Director and Club Secretary. All these people were now responsible to the Chief Executive, Chris Gorringe.

We did not have enough press vehicles for the amount of people now being allowed to travel. Again we pushed for more, or at least for a more realistic list of those allowed to use the press service.

We requested the Club should separate the passengers into two groups, players and VIPs, each group to leave separately from different departure points. This would not only quicken up the service but would control the bickering about who goes first, or so I hoped.

In 1987, which proved to be quite wet, one of the players said to the Press that he really looked forward to playing at Wimbledon but he felt it might be better if they held it in the summer.

The following year saw the International Box, which houses the overflow of dignitaries and overseas VIPs from the Royal Box, being re-sited on to the Centre Court while the old International Box was reallocated to the Last 8 Club. During these two years we trundled on, still with the same challenges to meet and the guest list rose again.

In 1989 the transport department moved from our comfortable, tented accommodation in Car Park 1 into the Link Building between the old and the new covered courts, hence the name 'Link'.

Before we moved into this building, which was certainly not intended to house a transport system, the Club should have undertaken certain adjustments. There should have been a separate telephone system, especially for transport. We had been running for 17 years, we were transporting well over a thousand people a day and we were still sharing the Club system which was impossible for such a busy department, and for the club's own operators who had to take all our calls and then transfer them to us. In the tented area we were vacating there was a comfortable area where people could wait for cars. In the Link building there was nothing but a tiny reception area with one sofa.

The Club had not given any thought to where the passengers would wait for transport so, as always, the passengers anxious to get into the cars first would not wait in the small reception area. The anxious ones waited outside which caused a very large crowd of people jostling for a seat in a car, and consequently the older people were pushed to the back.

When it rained they all became very tetchy and my controllers outside trying to control the crowd took a torrent of abuse. One lady controller had a large tennis bag thrown at her by one of the players which caught her head and nearly knocked her out. We had to send her off duty. In an unforgivable show of temper another of the tennis players spat in the face of the second controller and regrettably I had to report the behaviour to Alan Mills. The abuse was appalling and several controllers said they would not be returning the following year.

In addition to this aggravation the Club had agreed to supply two coaches as requested by lady players via the WTA. This was discussed at a meeting in Wimbledon in early 1989. Both the Chairman, John Curry, and I were very much against this as it was too inflexible. The majority of votes won and the WTA request was granted. It wasn't long into The Championships that the lady players refused to use the coaches and demanded cars instead. In addition the players, both male and female, kept refusing to share cars with the VIPs. I felt like knocking all their heads together.

Somehow we got through to the end of the tournament. I wrote a very stiff and long report to the transport sub-committee, which at least made me feel better. The other major thing that happened in 1989 was that the Club appointed a Television Marketing Director – my husband. I was not well pleased.

During 1990 we used 76 cars and 30 minibuses. We fitted 25 of the cars with radios which we were testing. We found them helpful in emergencies although our basic manual system, which I had installed all those years ago, was still performing very well.

As we got extra cars to cover the amount of people travelling the previous year we were shocked to learn that we were now transporting 1,500 people. Again this was more than the previous year so it still left an acute shortage of vehicles during our rush hours.

To avoid the unpleasantness of the previous year the Club had arranged for a tented area on the concourse in front of the covered courts, for passengers to comfortably wait for their transport home. When The Championships opened, the tented area was not ready for use and workmen were still crawling all over it. It took several days for this to be finished. When it was finished there was another problem. The stanchions of the marquee stuck out so far that only one line of cars could wait outside, and drivers in other cars returning from a run could not get past to check in to the main building. We ended up causing our own traffic jams and looking inefficient through no fault of our own.

This particular year the ATP (Association of Tennis Players) told the Club that the male players were to stay at The St.

James Court Hotel and that this should now be regarded as a new tournament hotel. I was surprised the Club could be dictated to in this way but they let it pass and we had to set up shop at The St. James.

It was a really good hotel but had little or no parking space. It was arranged that we should use an inner city school playground behind the minuscule parking space on offer at the hotel and that we should park our cars round the side of this. We were not allowed to enter during the children's break times and had to wait outside hoping to avoid the traffic wardens.

The pupils were not too keen on these arrangements and took great pleasure in playing chicken when the cars entered and they kicked their footballs at the heads of the drivers causing me to issue the instruction that all windows in the cars should remain shut, despite a lack of air conditioning.

This was also the year that in exasperation, due to the previous mishandling of Juniors, I offered to organise their transport too. I thought as I was always having to accommodate these teenagers I might as well manage the whole thing. The Club were pleased with this offer and Austin Rover were not expected to pay for it.

Austin Rover had supplied the girl drivers with very unsuitable satin dresses which made them look as if they were Marks and Spencer staff. The male drivers looked smart but the girls called their uniforms 'the nightdresses'.

The weather was really bad in the first week of 1991 and I understand that only about 9 hours of play were achieved in the first four days, due to rain, leaving 231 matches behind schedule.

It has been said to me on more than one occasion that once it rains we have nothing to do in transport. Not so. We were doubly busy as we had to run players in and out to practice areas, or into Wimbledon to check if their game had been postponed. The players were on edge and wanted to go up to Wimbledon village to chill or back to their hotels and then back to the courts again. When it rained we turned into a nanny service.

Because of this constant use during the day our cars ploughed up the ground which became a quagmire, causing bumps with cars, making our drivers overtired so they became frustrated and careless. The cars were parked in a field on grass with some cars dotted between trees. The area was very dark at night and the drivers became nervous of falling over tree roots as they searched for their cars. As all the cars were exactly the same bar the number plate this was no mean feat. Because of the mud we allowed the wearing of Wellingtons and to hell with the uniform.

This year also entailed working on the middle Sunday so the Referee could try to catch up on games. This was normally our only day off, although I had long felt that we should work on that day as the players still came in to practise and it was difficult for them to get out from Central London to Wimbledon without our help. Also having to work on this occasion threw our shift system out of sync. I sat up until midnight on the Saturday working out the new systems and unfortunately missed the LTA Ball to which I had been invited.

One of the most interesting years of all the tournaments I worked on at Wimbledon was in 1992. The Rover contract still had two years to run covering 1993 and 1994, as well as this year 1992. However 1992 was when they called a halt. The Club had consistently increased their demands of Rover by lengthening not only their guest list but also the days the transport system was expected to work. This meant more cars to accommodate Club guests over a longer period, which entailed costs to cover more drivers' salaries, more petrol, more insurance, and more driver food and National Insurance repayments.

It was not all the Club's fault and they fully expected Rover to ask for more of a financial contribution towards the following two years than the £40,000 plus VAT provided by the Club in 1992. This was to help towards the extra costs which Rover were having to meet, especially if the service was to be expanded yet again, and the drivers were to receive a more reasonable wage.

I was urged by the Club to press Rover for a more realistic rate of pay, though the Club stated that they had some misgivings that they might be asked to foot the bill themselves.

I was still the Club's official Transport Manager, for which I received an annual salary of unstartling proportions, so I was expected to carry out a few small negotiations on their behalf. This was not one that I relished, as I knew how Rover was viewing the situation.

On October 14th 1992 the Club officially thanked me at a meeting I attended for "her sterling contribution to The Championships and for her very thorough report". I was pleased to receive this accolade but concerned about the Rover situation. After all they were still my Client.

At the beginning of 1993 it was accepted that the Rover Car Company were not going to meet all their contractual obligations as far as the cost of the drivers and their ancillary costs was concerned. It was then decided that the Club should meet all those costs and I should take responsibility as Club Transport Manager to keep things running smoothly on the Club's behalf. It was decided that the Club would request 90 cars to be made available for the 3 weeks of Wimbledon beginning in 1993. This should relieve the pressure of running the service on the ground and make it more manageable.

The total costs rose by £34,117 between 1989 and 1992. The reasons, officially listed in a paper I sent to Richard Grier, at his request, were because of shortage of cars in 1990 the number of cars for the following year had risen to 70 (causing more staff costs). Also a marquee was erected for the reception of players and officials. In 1991 the cars were increased again from 70 to 90. The Press Park and Ride service and the public Park and Ride service both increased in size. Because more drivers were employed over these periods the administrative costs rose accordingly. Driver salary levels stayed the same and it was very difficult to find drivers of the right calibre at that level of salary. The Club took over the cost of the marquee, a fact Rover did not choose to recognise.

Although I was taking on yet more work for no more money, I felt that things were on the up. I was able to offer better facilities to passengers and in addition I had more cars to play with and could move people out of the Club more quickly and not crush too many people into a car which made their journeys more comfortable. Rover continued to supply the cars and their mechanics for the whole three weeks and things began at last to run more smoothly.

I should not forget the really bigger addition to the transport service on this particular year was that we were given a computer! It was used so much it was running on steam by the end of the tournament!

The Centenary of The Ladies Championship were celebrated in 1993. Although we had fairly good weather during these Championships it was quite rainy during the overseas week and this practice week ran through to the Sunday. As usual this put pressure on the cars over the weekend.

This was also the first year that the courtesy transport service had taken over the Junior operation. This should have been relatively painless as the Club had allowed us to ask Leyland Daf for 27 transits for the overall Junior service on the ground.

On the 14th June (my birthday, lucky me) 6 of the vehicles arrived. The further 21 vehicles began to arrive as arranged towards the end of overseas week (or practice week as we were now styling it because players from any area were now allowed to use the transport facilities). However Leyland Daf went into the hands of the Receiver. Oh joy! The Liquidator had sold off most of the vehicles scheduled for our use.

Leyland Daf asked the Club to consider that they be allowed to continue to work at Wimbledon as it was expected that there would soon be a management buyout. They contracted transit buses for us from a company called Chinfields. Because Chinfields was apparently covering a Ministry of Defence contract during the fortnight of Wimbledon they did not have enough buses to cover the contract. They therefore decided to contract the order out to another company. This other company then contracted our order out to a further company and by the time the transit buses arrived they were owned by no less than 10 companies.

As they all began arriving I stood outside the transport office with Robin Webb, my vehicles director and gave the vehicles a once-over. We had to return many of them because they were faulty. When the final two buses actually arrived one was towing the other. Robin and I had to laugh or we would have just cried. What to do – no buses? We managed to hire large 48-seater coaches to help us cope but as they were quite inflexible for our needs the service suffered. 1992 became known to us not as the Lady Champions year but the Year of the Buses.

Not to grumble however, because this year we were given a fax machine as well as a computer. It made us feel quite racy.

Security was now coming into the foreground. We had police approval over our emergency system which did not entirely tie up with that of the Club on the main ground but the police liked it well enough and told us to go ahead.

During 1993 I decided I was not going to work for such very long hours over a five-week period which my time at Wimbledon had now become without a little more remuneration for myself. So I gave the Club an ultimatum. Either I was paid a decent amount or I would not work for Wimbledon again. The Club shillied and shallied but finally came up with a higher figure for me but asked me to keep it to myself. The extra money was not what I had requested but it was an improvement so I decided to stay on at least until after the following year's tournament.

Nineteen-ninety-four was the year of Hertz First Service. This sponsorship deal had been brokered by Mark McCormack's company IMG. I understand Mark personally had made the suggestion to the Chairman of Hertz during an annual golf match which Mark organised for the chairmen of some very high powered international companies. For them it was a day off from the worries of running global industries and was, I understand, enjoyed by all.

When the deal was finalised it was tagged on to an agreement that Hertz could run advertisements on American television showing the perfect vehicle service being used at Wimbledon, the world's most prestigious tennis tournament. It was paid for by the American branch of Hertz with the European branch instigating the running of it.

Chris Gorringe, while being apprehensive about this, was relieved that the Club no longer had to pay for the transport service, but was nervous about how it would be run. He therefore insisted that Hertz sign a contract with my company to run the service on the ground in conjunction with Hertz.

During their first year at Wimbledon the Hertz staff were at sixes and sevens and appeared to be uncomfortable being there at all. They hung back and watched as we waded into our usual dance and more or less left us to it after having introduced themselves at the driver's briefing.

As this was a new company I decided that we would concentrate on logistics to give them some idea of what was going on. The statistics we took were pretty surprising.

Week 1	*Week 2*
40% VIPs	40% VIPs
22% Officials	40% Officials
38% Players	20% Players

Well! and I had thought this was supposed to be a Players' service. These figures shook the Club up a bit too. I hoped it would make them prune their lists a little and scratch off some of the, dare I say it, hangers-on.

This particular year the Service Stewards disgraced themselves, and not for the first time. The solution of the Club had been to close their bar earlier but the stewards continued to drink too much and fight with each other while going home on our buses. They climbed over the driver's seat while the vehicle was in motion and generally played 'chicken' which was very dangerous.

Our recommendation – relieve the passengers of their Club accreditation card at the beginning of the journey and only return it when they reached their destination if they had behaved during the journey. Without it they could not get in to Wimbledon. We also recommended two large and brawny controllers to fill the buses at the start of the journey and two more at the end of the journey to keep a check on things. Bus drivers were leaving us in droves because of these goings on. The upshot was – well guess. The Club continued to close the bar earlier.

Hertz decided to take staff photographs which I made my co-director Val Ward take part in. My excuse, I was too busy applying steaks to two black eyes on a service steward.

The following year I signed the first contract I had ever signed for transport. It was between Hertz and Gemini for five years. I had never signed a contract with Rover as I did a great deal of other work with them and they knew they would get a good job at a good price. My association to the point when Rover left Wimbledon had been good for twenty years. In the future I was to work for them again on transport but for a very different client.

Although the Club had appointed me their transport manager in 1975 I had never actually had a contract. They did however have a badge made for me to wear with Wimbledon Transport Manager printed on it. I still have it somewhere in my possession. Having a contract means you can breathe for five years without having that slight worry that the client will want a change. It also means that you can plan ahead. It was a good feeling.

By 1996 Hertz were already looking to curb the costs of the transport service. During the second week of The Championships they cut the amount of cars from 90 (180) drivers to 70 cars (140) drivers until the final Sunday when it returned to its original numbers in order to service the Champions Dinner at the Savoy Hotel. As this was done at the last minute we had to lay off drivers and ask them to come back on the Sunday night. There were some very angry drivers that year.

The cars Hertz used were Ford Galaxies, a perfectly serviceable vehicle. The Club guests, however, did not think much of them and felt they were being transported "in a van", especially after Rover's top-notch limousines. Some of the lady VIPs refused to get in them at all until they realised there was nothing else. We, of course, liked them as they had seven seats as opposed to five and we were moving the crowds in record time.

The Hertz Ford Transits were much smaller than the Leyland Daf Sherpas. At this stage Hertz were only supplying 11-seaters as opposed to the Daf 15 and 18-seater buses.

In 1997 the luggage van appeared. This van was like a removal van and was used to take the heavy bags the players travel the world with instead of us having to remove seats from cars to accommodate the luggage. Although it isn't handsome it is my favourite vehicle on the whole fleet.

Hertz were keen to deliver all vehicles early despite Club requests to stick to our schedules, as frankly we had nowhere to put them. As grass had to be cut and bays painted, this meant that Gemini executive staff had to keep shifting cars about in order to let the gardeners do their job, and needless to say we got the flak too.

This year we had prepared our own training films so the driver training was more comprehensive. We are living in interesting times and security is very important as far as vehicles are concerned. I had learned a lot about security at the G7 Summit when we had been responsible for numerous heads of state and their entourages.

At Wimbledon we were responsible for high earning players and some very important guests, sometimes including Royals. Our training was conducted by ex-police officers with talks by the local constabulary as well. Our accident rate was so low we had a better quote from the insurance people in 1987 because of it.

I thought that the drivers who had been dressed by Hertz in yellow and black stripes looked like bumble bees and it kept me smiling throughout the tournament. We had a very young Hertz representative who was impossible to work with but I felt her efforts at uniforms must show some sort of sense of humour.

This year it rained very heavily throughout the tournament and our cars were continually having to be towed out of the mud by the AA. My vehicles director, Robin Webb, had his work cut out keeping the cars on the road.

This year the first day of The Championships was known as Black Monday. By mid-morning we had completely run out of cars, apart from those still being towed by the AA. The new Number 1 Court opened officially on that day and everyone was anxious to travel in for the festivities.

In order to meet Hertz requests to cut costs we had dropped ten drivers. This left us very short all day and I vowed next year that ten drivers would be back. We did have a lot of sympathy from the passengers who were appreciative of our efforts over this difficult fortnight, so we came out smiling after all.

In 1998 we suffered two tube strikes and very wet weather conditions in practice week. Poor weather delays during the

Qualifying Tournament, held at the Bank of England sports ground, caused the Referee to divide the competitors into two groups and send them to different venues. The extra venue, which was used by the ladies' group, at Chiswick watered down the transport service to an alarming degree and we almost came unstuck.

This year we got radios for the cars which I was initially dubious about but which proved to be invaluable. We were asked to start the staff Park and Ride service at 6 a.m. in order to accommodate catering staff. In order to avoid driver overtime we used a rolling rota system. The service ran until 11.30 p.m.

A Government white paper was published which included concerns on the safety of not only 18-seater vehicles but also 15-seaters. This caused us to hotfoot it to the Weigh Station in Croydon to ensure our loads were within the existing limits.

Of particular concern was the Airport Service when the players carried a lot of heavy luggage. Boris Becker once used two minibuses to move his family's belongings. I joked with his wife Barbara asking what she had bought – she loved shopping. "Oh no," she said, "we take Noah's" (their son) "nursery with us so he feels at home with all the travelling to different venues." I was pleased we now had a furniture van working for us and contemplated asking for a second one just in case all the other player dads and mums decided to do the same.

On this particular year when our vehicles arrived in Wimbledon they contained only enough petrol to unload them off the transporters onto the grounds of Wimbledon. This obliged Gemini instructors to make many visits to the petrol station with cans in order to put enough petrol into each official vehicle to enable them to be driven to the garage to fill up. The legal amount of petrol a vehicle can contain on a transporter is 2 gallons. We do not know why Hertz delivered them virtually empty but it took us all day to complete the job. The Press got wind of this which reflected badly on Hertz in the nationals the following morning. It never happened again!

107

This was to be the last year in our present offices. In the year 2000 it was planned that we should move into our new offices which were presently being built under Plan 2 of the grand plan for the grounds of Wimbledon. The players were to catch their transport out of the new area, the VIPs were to get a smartened-up version of the present marquee. This is what I had been working on and waiting for, for too long.

Chapter 6

THE NEW MILLENNIUM

The year 2000 was for me a double-edged sword. First our new chairman of the transport sub-committee was Julian Tatum, Lord Kindersley having sadly retired the year before. Julian was, it appeared, genuinely keen to be working in transport. From what he said, it seemed he had been involved in running a fleet of transport for another tennis tournament. I did not realise it was a fleet of only 30 minibuses on a shuttle service and, according to members of the Club who had used it, it had not worked well.

For now I was pleased by his enthusiasm, and the fact that he said his intention was to put much more money into the service to attain the standard I had been working towards for so long. He even invited me to lunch in the member's enclosure on my birthday which fell in the middle of June.

At this point I was impressed by him although I had loved working with Hugo Kindersley. For the Millennium it was decided to celebrate by inviting as many Wimbledon Champions as were still alive and available for the tournament. I understand that the Club met fares and accommodation for each of them. 64 singles and doubles champions agreed to come and as a result we hired two extra 27-seater buses to accommodate the extra usage.

This year we moved half of the transport service from the Link Building to the new building within the grounds of the All

England Club to deal with players' requirements from their new premises. The areas we were allocated as offices did not function well for us and in my annual report sent to the Club after the event I complained snippily that the architecture should have been functionally led as from an operating point of view it did not work for us.

It was, however, a great improvement for the competitors. They now had their own area and entrance/exit without the VIPs. It should be noted too that the Club had a new member's area which was very large and luxurious. We had a room as large as a cupboard and the hatch area through which we were to deal with player's bookings, while in existence, could not be opened because of fire regulations!

In front of the players' building, where the cars collected the players when they left the Club, the space was very tight and the cars had to use single file which slowed the whole service down as we had always used double lanes. In addition the kerbs were large and impractical. In the first week alone we had the side of 12 tyres damaged.

The exit gate onto Somerset Road was no better as the kerbs were lined up with the gate and not the oncoming traffic, so again we were catching the side of tyres, the weakest part, as the cars moved out on to the road. This was all altered the year following after the Club had received my report on it, but it caused a lot of problems when it opened.

The good part was the players and VIPs were at last separated and the traffic flowed well as no one tried to take precedence over anyone else. This was what I had been waiting for and the new systems we adapted were working well.

We also had a new part-computerisation of the booking service which had been taken from my original service manual and transformed into a quicker system which now worked very well. It speeded up the bookings from two-and-a-half minutes manually to thirty seconds on the computerised version. It was well done and I was very pleased with the programmer and the programme.

We had many compliments from both the VIPs who loved their new spruced-up lounge in the old marquee, and from the players who loved the freedom of their new lounge and all the new facilities. We also had very kind words from the American Chairman of Hertz Europe, Charles Shafer, who was now overseeing the service himself from Hertz point of view and was a delight to work with.

However the greatest compliment of all came from the record breaking Champion himself, Pete Sampras, when he singled out transport for praise in his speech at the Champions Dinner at the Savoy Hotel on the final Sunday. It was a proud moment for me after all the blood, sweat and tears that went into the running of the transport system over the early days.

Everything looked set fair for the next few years and I signed the new five-year contract with Hertz with a light heart. But... fairly soon a bombshell was about to fall which shattered my relationship with the Club.

Julian Tatum visited Gemini Two offices in October 2000 with some proposals which I found unacceptable. So much so that I spoke to my solicitor who advised me to write to Julian and ask for a written explanation of his intentions because the implications of what he was proposing were so serious.

As I was under contract to Hertz, the sponsors, it was obvious that I was keeping them as Clients for the next five years. Julian's proposals for me to run the tournament from my own offices and to send the rest of my staff to work alone on the grounds of Wimbledon did not make sense.

His letter in reply to mine was along the lines that what he wanted me to do, and he assured me that I would be in a 'win-win' situation if I agreed to his proposals, was for me not to appear at Wimbledon. This was ridiculous and I said I had no intention of breaking my contract with Hertz which was to run the service on the ground. As the Chairman of the Transport sub-committee he had the authority to make changes to the running of the transport service. He did not have any authority to change the contract my company held with my Client.

Things appeared to calm down and I did not have any contact with Julian, nor indeed the Club until our next scheduled transport sub-committee meeting which was held at the All England Club and chaired by the new Wimbledon chairman, Tim Phillips. It was attended by the relevant sub-committee members, myself and Hertz.

At the meeting, held in November I was very apprehensive as to its outcome. I had no idea of who knew of the meeting in my offices or of Julian's intentions. I felt nervous and isolated. However, before I entered the committee room, the Hertz representative Roy Ritnour who was managing the Hertz side of the contract, attending the meeting with the Hertz Chairman, Charles Shafer, took me to one side. "Don't worry, just keep your head down, he" (referring to Julian) "is a very vain man." I realised my Client had been informed of what was going on and how they felt about it and I entered the meeting with a little more confidence.

For me it turned out to be quite harrowing, although the committee praised me for the way the tournament had been handled from the transport end which I believed had been the best we had ever done. I remember however that when stating some facts, I was so nervous I began to stumble over my words. Charles Shafer, Hertz Chairman, finished the sentence for me, for which I was very grateful.

I had no support for my position from the Club's officers, possibly because they already realised that it was a *fait accompli*. I do not think Julian gave a thought to how much he had upset me then or since. During the following few years he systematically set about trivialising my position at Wimbledon to such an extent that it made my situation there untenable. 2001 to 2004 were the unhappiest years I had spent at The Championships and it has taken me a long time to recover from them.

However, I learned that Roy Ritnour was going back to America and he was being replaced by Janet Dicks who was the Hertz Director of Franchise. We had met before to discuss other business Hertz might put my way and I had liked her as soon as we met. We had a very friendly working relationship during my latter years at Wimbledon and it was her sense of humour and the fact that she was not afraid to roll her sleeves up when we were busy that were in such direct contrast to Julian that I found her presence there quite refreshing. Charles Shafer too was very kind and helpful so at least on one side we had a good working relationship.

Despite all the unpleasantness, the next tournament loomed ahead of us so it was back to work. It had been decided at that fateful meeting that the transport operation was outgrowing its environs so in addition to the VIPs' marquee it was proposed by the sub-committee that the managers and telephonists should move into a Portakabin outside the covered courts.

The Portakabin they hired was too small and did not work well at all. Julian had appointed a friend to manage the operation. His name was Roy Just. He had informed me of this in a letter which told me that Hertz were going to also try to place a manager at Wimbledon. This was confusing as Janet followed Roy Ritnour and there had never been a gap in someone from Hertz attending Wimbledon.

We appeared to be all chiefs and no Indians. Poor Roy, he was in very close contact with us all, sitting in that tiny hot Portakabin and protesting (his words) that he wasn't there to spy on us. I noticed however he was carefully watching everything we did and noting it all down on his computer for use in his later report to the Club. No one took much notice of him as we were all busy with our own very busy jobs. I felt quite sorry for him.

He protested to me the job was not what he had expected and he would not do it another year, but I knew he would. He was a good tennis player and it was a prestige position for him to work at Wimbledon. He wouldn't give that up in a hurry.

Julian drew up a new plan. After thirty years, and the two years I had run the service single-handed for both the Club and Rover, and having been appointed the Club's transport manager, I was no longer to take part in the sub-committee meetings. Roy Just was to take my place and had been appointed by Julian as Transport Coordinator for the All England Club. I was to attend a new meeting, as was Roy, which was a 'transport working meeting' and Roy was to be its representative at the main Transport sub-committee meeting.

The working meeting was to be chaired by Richard Grier, Championships Director and attended by two Wimbledon managers – Richard Oxborrow, Championships Coordinator and John Cox the Club's Maintenance Manager. Janet Dicks of Hertz also attended with some of her staff. I called in Robin Webb, my vehicles director, and my secretary to take notes. It was a useful enough meeting but extra really to what we had always had, and it took even longer to get things done, as requests had to go through two committees rather than just one.

I consoled myself that up to now I had been lucky to have the privilege of working with John Curry and Lord Kindersley when they were Chairmen of the transport sub-committee and I decided that I would just get on with my job of running transport as I had always done.

Getting 2001 right under Julian's directives was a challenge. It was an unusually busy year. Our Portakabin was infested with ants in the good weather and it leaked around the doors when it rained. The players liked to visit even though it was small and already had 12 occupants trying to work, as they were used to coming in our offices for a chat and the VIPs also visited to socialise, complain or ask the name of the best restaurant around.

There were rats in the bushes outside which frightened some of the ladies and I suspect some of the men too. There was nowhere to take staff for a private word when the need arose. The phones did not work for the first three days which drove the players to despair.

Roy Just submitted the drivers and managers to close questioning in his bid to arm himself with information, which caused an atmosphere among the staff. Even our old offices with loose wires and no light looked good after this.

One of Julian's new directives was for drivers to telephone in from the car with a 'POB' call (passenger on board), the old taxi cry. Robin, the radio operators and I all warned against it but Roy insisted it was Julian's wish, so against our better judgement we went ahead. We had 90 cars, doing approximately three pickups from central London during our morning rush hour between 9 a.m. and 12 noon. That meant approximately 273 pob calls due in approximately three hours on one line. Of course the lines jammed and other urgent calls, such as accidents, breakdowns or failed pickups could not always get through.

Although I was trying to keep out of the way this year, I had to step in and stop it. Three furious letters from two radio controllers and one driver who had had an emergency were attached to my 2001 annual report to Hertz, who were horrified that the idea had been put forward in the first place.

The kitchen area where the driver's food was prepared by our four sandwich-makers was dirty. My assistant and I spent a morning before anyone arrived cleaning it thoroughly. We found a lot of white powder on the shelves and the floor. We cleaned it off.

On opening one of the drawers we found a packet of white powder with 'Rat Poisoning' on the front cover. This meant that had we not used that drawer and had not cleaned up the white powder we would have been including it in the driver's sandwiches. As cleaning the building was the Club's responsi-

115

bility I addressed my rather stiff Health and Safety form to them. This really was not a good year.

In May 2002 I visited Paris and while there I went to the Roland Garros stadium to watch the French Grand Slam. Wandering around the grounds I noticed that the press offices were housed in two storied marquees and were very comfortable for the staff working in them. I took some photographs of the marquees and brought them back to show the Club. The Championships Director, Richard Grier liked my idea of scrapping the uncomfortable Portakabin and erecting a two-storey marquee with the VIPs' lounge on the ground floor and our offices above.

Julian was duly consulted and he too approved the idea, so it went ahead. For once my staff and I were very comfortably housed with decent offices and equipment and all our computers, printers and the fax machine were all kept in a small partitioned-off area leading from our main office. And guess what, the telephones worked too.

I had also looked carefully at the facilities provided at the Qualifying competition and put forward my ideas to the Club. Within reason they accommodated us there as well. Julian was keeping his word about putting money into the service and this financial help was improving all our facilities which made our work easier.

Unfortunately Julian merely nodded to me when we met although he managed a word when there were people around. It hurt, but I did not lose any sleep over it.

In 2003 it was noticeable that travelling patterns were changing. The players were getting familiar with their new settings and were beginning to use the facilities. They now had an excellent gym and restaurant in their building and also an Internet room for them to use, and the habit of 'hanging out' or 'chilling' in the Club's environs became more popular. Therefore instead of just coming in for practice or their match or to have their rackets strung, they were coming in to enjoy their new surroundings.

116

We had to cope with the huge demands this made on the cars in the mornings, when people other than players were making demands on the service also. I decided that in the following year I would bring on the 20 empty airport cars earlier in the week to cope with demand. These cars were not needed until the Wednesday of the first week as not many had lost their matches and needed to get to the airport. Hertz liked this proposal but the Club hummed and hawed because they had to pay for the extra drivers, insurance, petrol etc.

Hertz had been clever, or I should say Charles Shafer had been long-sighted in saying that he had a budget which he agreed with the Club and he would not spend over this set amount. Any extras the Club needed they should pay for.

1,533 names were entered in the computer as being eligible for travel in 2003. The booking system was working well and this year we had computerised the airport system as well. So Hertz were certainly footing a large bill.

This year also saw the start of Ken Livingstone's congestion charging in the centre of London. Although I personally approved of the idea, it was a challenge as we were not exempt from it. After the mix-up over VAT payments I wonder if the Olympic Committee have thought of this extra cost if they are not exempted in 2012.

This was quite a challenge and I thought long and hard about how much it would cost to register our 110 cars. The buses were exempt at that time because they had more than 9 seats, so the park and ride systems were safe for now.

Under normal circumstances, we used the cars for 21 days and 6 of the cars for a further week for training purposes. Our London hotels were in the congestion zone so this too had to be taken into consideration.

The plan I came up with was not the easiest one for us as operators to deal with but it did save the Club a great deal of money. I had large, white sticky labels printed with a big red 'C' on each and stuck them in the windows of 20 cars per day which were to be used as congestion cars. I appointed a full-time congestion controller with experience of running and scheduling vehicles.

I based the operation at our transport desk at the Gloucester Hotel and made sure that those cars were used for central London runs only. As the drivers preferred to work out of Wimbledon where all the excitement of the tournament was, I made sure that the drivers changed daily and everyone had a go at being a congestion car. Thanks to the congestion manager's efforts this worked well, although my secretary and a controller had to telephone to register the cars at night when they had been chosen so they did not think much of the idea.

We ran several Park and Ride bus services but unfortunately the Club decided that we should cease to run the Public Park and Ride because we had to hire buses. Another company who ran the service from Wimbledon station to the Club had buses to spare and could afford to run it more cheaply.

I was disappointed because I had enjoyed working on bus projects more than cars but I realised it would save a lot of money. However, Roy Just was put in charge of running it and I felt he had no sense of urgency so Robin and I kept an eye on it and had on many occasions to go out and clear the crowds as Roy was elsewhere at the time.

Our Staff Park and Ride transported 10,547 people over 13 days in 6 nine-seater transits. Busy indeed!

The next year, 2004, was to be my last year at Wimbledon although I did not realise it then. It was the final year of my five-year contract with Hertz. It is pleasant to look back over all the letters, notes, flowers, good wishes from the very many passengers who travelled that year, some of whom I am still in touch with.

The year, however, held a few challenges. Julian Tatum came up with another of his ideas, which we had no choice but to follow. We had brought to the notice of the Club that players leaving Wimbledon for the States and Australia etc. needed their airport cars during the night as opposed to the evening. Our service finished at midnight and started at 8.00 a.m. Some players needed a car at 11 p.m. and we had been asked for cars around 4 a.m. in the morning to catch 6 a.m. flights.

The drivers allocated these times were extremely tired because they had to work an 8-hour day on top of that. We asked for overtime pay to be raised but the Club turned this down. Julian suggested using a taxi service overnight. This seemed worth looking into but Julian suggested a company that he knew would be able to do the job.

We met up with the taxi service he suggested and they did indeed agree that the job would be no problem for them to cover. We painted as black a picture as we could to make sure they knew what it was like to deal with players. They were quite willing to give it a go and assured us nothing would go wrong.

I said I would like to monitor their calls each night as I was worried about the tennis players being left behind when they had tournaments in other countries to go to. Having travelled to several countries with the players, I knew what a nightmare it could be. We had been taking about 40 of these calls a night which we had told the taxi company.

They only did the job for two nights and called a halt saying they had to deal with their own clients and could only cover two calls a night. We later discovered they were basically a one-man band.

Roy Just tried to rescue the situation and suggested another company. They could take on no more 6 calls a night. Had I researched this I could have come up with a solution, but that had been taken out of my hands. I wonder how this problem progressed after I left. The cars were idle overnight. More drivers employed by the transport service could have covered these problems if only the Club had agreed to pay them. Perhaps Julian had another bright solution.

Chapter 7

TO BID OR NOT TO BID –
THAT IS THE QUESTION.

In 2004 Julian Tatum announced that with the cooperation of Neil Cunningham (now the manager representing Hertz at Wimbledon, in place of Charles Shafer who had returned to work in America in 2003), that the transport service at Wimbledon should be put out to tender as soon as the last contract finished.

This was a bitter blow to me. 2004 was my thirty-second year managing the transport system for the All England Club at their Championships, using the system I had created in my own time and developed over the years. It was a very successful one and because of its success it had opened up opportunities for me to develop transport systems for sporting events all over the world.

I felt this was Julian's way of seeing me off. I discovered that one of my competitors was bidding. If Julian had any sense and he really didn't want me around personally, was sure he would accept their bid, as they were a very competent company. Roy Just and Janet Dicks were to interview the companies who were bidding.

I worked out a strategy and costings with my then right-hand assistant, which she typed for me, and then I went on my annual holiday. The bid documents were sent out to me in Spain by Janet Dicks who was keen for me to continue doing the job. I often find on holiday you tend to relax and begin to see things in a different light. I read the documents and put them to one side to enjoy my holiday.

I had noted that Julian would be deciding how many cars would be used based on the previous year's figures on the computer. Logic did not always follow Julian's enthusiasm and I could see this would lead to more tricky situations. However, I still had time to make a decision so I put the documents to one side.

When I returned to my office I took out the bid documents and re-read them. My assistant was not there and when I called her she told me she was ill. This gave me more time to decide what to do.

Financially I did not need to work. If I did bid and was chosen it would mean being contracted for another five years. I had not enjoyed the last five years so that did not appeal to me. My husband Ian had retired from the Club two years previously and we had lots of plans about what we wanted to do in the future. Besides I did not think I could stomach working for five more years with Julian, or even Roy.

I would miss the camaraderie with the drivers, and the controllers, and some players and VIPs and the sheer excitement of being around a great world famous event and running the transport system I had worked so hard on. Even though it was copyrighted to me I had always intended to leave it with the Club when I retired. Also my bid might not be successful and that would not only be humiliating but extremely hurtful after my long association and loyalty to the Club. Did I really want to put myself in that position? My staff would receive redundancy if I closed the company and as both were competent if mature secretaries/assistants I did not see a problem with them finding employment elsewhere.

So I took the momentous decision and I did not put in a bid.

I had a call from Janet Dicks of Hertz to meet her for a drink. She was sorry I had not put in a bid and felt she would really not want to represent Hertz at Wimbledon now. She told me that my competitor's bid had been too expensive for the Club and that my own two permanent staff had put in a bid of their own which had been accepted.

I was surprised that they had not told me about this but I asked Janet why they had been chosen. "Julian and Neil wanted continuity," she said. Still I am sure they will get as good a service as they have always had. They are using my system, and running the transport system now is like painting by numbers. I am sure the girls will put their own stamp on it and Julian of course has nothing to worry about.

In 2005 the Club invited me, with my husband, to be their guests in the Royal Box. Unfortunately we had booked our annual holiday to cover the period of Wimbledon in case I had second thoughts, which luckily I didn't. Sadly we had to turn down this prestigious invitation.

I still visit the Club for dinner on rare occasions which helps me catch up with some old friends and some of the executives now retired as well. In retrospect it was the right time for me to leave. A lot of the people who worked with me have retired and I still see Richard Grier and Richard Oxborrow too. No, we don't really talk about Wimbledon – we have other things to do.

And, as I said at the beginning it was all Hughie Green's fault!